CHILDREN SPEAK FOR THEMSELVES

Using the Kempe Interactional Assessment to Evaluate Allegations of Parent-Child Sexual Abuse

CHILDREN SPEAK FOR THEMSELVES

Using the Kempe Interactional Assessment to Evaluate Allegations of Parent-Child Sexual Abuse

By

Clare Haynes-Seman, Ph.D.
Associate Professor
C. Henry Kempe National Center for the
Prevention and Treatment of Child Abuse and Neglect
Department of Pediatrics
University of Colorado Health Sciences Center

David Baumgarten, J.D.
Gunnison County Attorney
Gunnison, Colorado

BRUNNER/MAZEL *Publishers* • New York

Library of Congress Cataloging-in-Publication Data

Haynes-Seman, Clare
    Children speak for themselves: using the Kempe interactional assess-
ment to evaluate allegations of parent-child sexual abuse/by Clare
Haynes-Seman and David Baumgarten.
        p.   cm.
    Includes bibliographical references and index.
        ISBN 0-87630-745-4
    1. Incest victims.   2. Sexually abused children.   3. Family assessment.
4. Interviewing in child abuse.   I. Baumgarten, David.   II.Title.
HV6570.6.H39   1994
362.7'6—dc20   94-10231
                                                           CIP

Published by
BRUNNER/MAZEL, INC.
19 Union Square West
New York, New York 10003

Manufactured in the United States of America
10 9 8 7 6 5 4 3 2 1

To Heather
and all of the children
who demonstrated to us that
children can and do
speak for themselves
about sexual abuse.

"*If mankind had been able to learn from a direct observation of children, these three essays could have remained unwritten.*"

—SIGMUND FREUD
([1920/1953] in his Preface to the Fourth Edition
of *Three Essays on the Theory of Children*)

"*History, despite its wrenching pain, cannot be unlived, but if faced with courage need not be lived again.*"

—MAYA ANGELOU
([1993] from "On the Pulse of Morning")

Contents

Preface

Clinical and legal professionals struggle daily with fundamental challenges presented by allegations that a parent has sexually abused a child. Professionals are required to accurately determine whether the sexual abuse occurred and, if so, whether a particular parent is the perpetrator. Cases in which it is recognized, with definitive evidence demonstrating that the abuse occurred, and with an identifiable perpetrator are the exceptions rather than the rule.

A parent's confession to sexually abusing a child is rare. Typically, there are no eyewitnesses. Direct physical and medical evidence of sexual abuse, even when available, seldom identify the specific perpetrator. Often, the determination of whether and by whom sexual abuse of a child was committed depends on the existence of a direct verbal disclosure of the child (Everson & Boat, 1989). Tragically, children who do not or cannot make such a direct verbal disclosure may remain at risk. Professionals require a clinical procedure that not only accurately accesses information, but also helps to uncover and verify the abuse.

Professionals are additionally challenged because the allegation—and if true, the abuse—occurs within the context of family relationships. If the abuse occurred and the perpetrator is a parent, the professionals are asked to conduct a course of therapy to attempt to heal the relationship. Professionals are in dire need of an assessment procedure that can form the basis for such treatment. If the sexual abuse did not occur, or if the parent was not the perpetrator, the professionals must attempt to

preserve the family relationships. Such an assessment procedure should be the first step in this healing effort.

Professionals are further challenged because the assessment
process must not only be clinically reliable, but also must often
meet and withstand the rigors of increasingly adversarial legal
proceedings.

There is, however, an effective and accepted method available that provides a solution to the above-cited fundamental assessment challenges. The Kempe Interactional Assessment has
been used successfully in difficult and complex cases involving
allegations of parent-child sexual abuse. This assessment procedure conducted in the conceptual framework of family attachment relationships includes a clinical interview of each parent
in the presence of the child, videotaped observations of parent-
child interactions, and an individual play interview with the child.
The basics of the Kempe Interactional Assessment for Parent-
Child Sexual Abuse make it uniquely suited to meet assessment
challenges.

First, is the fact that children, even preverbal and nonverbal
children, speak for themselves about experiences with important persons in their lives. Interactional assessment, by accurately recognizing, understanding, and translating children's
speech, makes available for clinical and legal professionals crucial, firsthand information that might otherwise be ignored.

Second, because an allegation or actual occurrence of
parent-child sexual abuse takes place in the context of family
relationships, it necessarily affects and is affected by those relationships. Observable interactions in nonsexually abusive family relationships can be differentiated reliably from those
observed in sexually abusive family relationships. The Kempe
Interactional Assessment affords crucial clinical data about the
qualities and dynamics of the family relationships. It provides

definitive data about the validity of an allegation of sexual abuse by a parent of a child in that family.

Third, one can be trained to be an accurate observer and translator of children's speech and family behavior. A presentation by a person skilled in interactional assessment is effective and can be relied upon in adversarial legal proceedings.

Children Speak for Themselves presents the history, rationale, protocol, and academic bases for the Kempe Interactional Assessment for Parent-Child Sexual Abuse. It provides clear models that differentiate why and how children speak and families behave in nonsexually abusive and sexually abusive relationships. It delineates the skills that must be obtained and the tasks that must be completed for one to use interactional assessment accurately and effectively. Case illustrations are presented that show the value of interactional assessment and the advantages of integrating it into a multidisciplinary peer review process. Evidentiary and practical considerations for court presentation are discussed.

There are increasing demands on clinicians and legal professionals to provide accurate assessment and definitive evidence regarding allegations of parent-child sexual abuse. The Kempe Interactional Assessment for Parent-Child Sexual Abuse meets those demands.

Foreword

In this pioneering book, Clare Haynes-Seman and David Baumgarten describe a technique of interactional assessment that is particularly useful for evaluation and clarification in difficult, emotionally laden, complex cases of alleged sexual abuse of a child by a parent or parent figure. Such cases are entering our legal system in increasing numbers, often in the course of custody disputes.

Laws mandating the reporting of child abuse were first passed in Colorado in 1964, soon after the magnitude of physical abuse and neglect of infants and young children had been brought to public attention. The purpose was to enable society to bring under care and protection the enormous number of battered and neglected children who at that time were unknown, unrecognized, and uncared for. In recent decades the awareness of sexual abuse has burgeoned and has been reported with the same purpose of providing care and protection for hurt children.

In our culture people are more emotionally disturbed by sexual abuse, especially of children, than they are by other antisocial and criminal behaviors. They deplore, but in a way accept as inevitable parts of life, the abundance of assault and battery, robbery, fraud, and manslaughter reported daily in our media. Child sexual molestation arouses much more horror, moral outrage, religious anathema, and vindictiveness. In a different way, some people find aberrant, tabooed sexual behavior so abhorrent that they deny even the possibility of its existence, especially in the case of citizens who seem respectable.

Typically a parent reports to authorities that a child has complained about sexual molestation by the other parent (usually the father). The child is examined medically and questioned by law enforcement and social services about the allegations. Even if abuse has occurred, there may be no physical symptoms, and the child's statements may be unavailable or confusing.

Despite all the uncertainties and confusion, it is still important to determine what, if anything, has happened to the child. The sexual abuse, or false allegation of abuse, may not be the real problem; they can be inappropriate attempts to solve problems in already dysfunctional family relationships. Such situations are not likely to arise in normally healthy family interactions.

It is generally recognized that family members interact with each other in relatively consistent ways. Thus it becomes useful to talk to the parents and to observe for several hours the interactions and attachment behaviors between child and parents in several contexts.

Without the pressure of directly questioning the child, the Kempe Interactional Assessment for Parent-Child Sexual Abuse allows the emergence of a different kind of data. The child can express in nonverbal behavior and spontaneous talk much that has not been evident in direct confrontation and examinations. Sexual abuse is not a sudden mysterious event appearing out of nowhere. Rather it is an event in the total life histories of perpetrator and child, derived from patterns of interaction developed in previous life experiences.

Children learn their verbal language, the "mother tongue," in interaction with their early-year caregivers. They also learn a nonverbal "language" of behavioral communications in the same relationship. The observation of the subtle nonverbal behavior of an allegedly sexually abused child with each parent can reveal much about how he or she has experienced them and what he or she feels and knows but is not able to tell in words.

A FEW CAVEATS

The purpose of the assessment is to gain information that will be most useful in promoting the welfare of the child, not just to prove which parent is right or wrong or more deserving, nor to find a "quick-fix" solution to a complicated problem of human relationships. The assessor cannot be an amateur. The task requires experience with all forms of abuse, good knowledge of child development, attachment theory, healthy child-rearing, basic psychological and psychiatric knowledge, and, most of all, an ability to be patient, tolerant, and curious without any pre-conceptions or bias about what one will find. Training is necessary in what kind of things to look for, how to listen, how to understand what one sees and hears, and how to integrate these components with all other available information. It is a demanding task, not to be undertaken lightly. *Children Speak for Themselves* gives us a remarkable picture of how to explore the intricacies of conflicted human behavior.

BRANDT F. STEELE, M.D.
Psychoanalyst and Professor Emeritus,
C. Henry Kempe National Center for
the Prevention and Treatment of
Child Abuse and Neglect,
Department of Psychiatry,
University of Colorado Health
Sciences Center

Acknowledgments

We acknowledge the clinical work of Patrick Bacon, M.D.; Diane Baird, M.S.W., L.C.S.W.; Jane Hoffmann, R.N., M.S.; David P. H. Jones, M.D.; Michele Kelly, Psy.D.; Tammy Perry, M.S.W.; and Beth Trimmer, R.N., M.S. These individuals participated in the evaluations of children who were eager to communicate their experiences but needed someone to listen and to understand what they were communicating.

We gratefully acknowledge the pioneering work of Dr. C. Henry Kempe, Dr. Ruth Kempe, and Dr. Brandt F. Steele, who recognized that one could learn a great deal about healthy and unhealthy parent-child relationships by talking with parents and by observing them with their children. We also acknowledge the contributions of Christy Cutler and Janet Dean, who worked with Dr. Ruth Kempe in developing an interview and observation protocol that was the prototype for the interactional assessment.

In acknowledgment of their roles and the roles of many others at the C. Henry Kempe National Center for the Prevention and Treatment of Child Abuse and Neglect, the procedure described in this book for the evaluation of allegations of parent-child sexual abuse is referred to as the "Kempe Interactional Assessment for Parent-Child Sexual Abuse."

CHILDREN SPEAK FOR THEMSELVES

Using the Kempe Interactional Assessment to Evaluate Allegations of Parent-Child Sexual Abuse

1

How to Turn a Problem into a Solution

A professional who seeks to make an accurate determination of whether a parent has sexually abused a child is confronted by a host of difficult and seemingly insurmountable obstacles. Many of these obstacles are presented by the real and complex dynamics of familial sex abuse. Many of these obstacles, however, may be self-imposed by an affirmatively narrow consideration of information from the rich and useful range available.

Assessing an accusation of parent-child sexual abuse in the conceptual framework of family attachment relationships permits one to make beneficial use of the family dynamics rather than be stymied by them and requires one to gather and consider all available information rather than to ignore some details.

An accusation or conduct of parent-child sexual abuse occurs within a family and permeates all the relationships in the family. In both cases family relationships are not healthy. Although one important focus of the assessment is the unique relationship between the accused parent and the child, including any evidence of specific incidents of alleged abuse, a complete assessment requires an examination of all the family attachment relationships since these will provide additional, relevant information that the examination of an individual parent-child relationship will not.

An evaluator must accept the dismaying facts of nondisclosure by child victims, the paucity of confessions by perpetrators, and the lack of generalized behaviors specific to children who have been sexually abused. But an evaluator must take advantage of those real and identifiable patterns of behavior that assessment of attachment relationships provides.

HEALTHY AND UNHEALTHY ATTACHMENT RELATIONSHIPS

Attachment theory integrates principles of psychoanalytic, social learning, and animal behavior theory to explain how the initial bond between infant and mother develops and serves as the precursor of the infant's future interactions with others. A primary, secure, and harmonious attachment between infant and mother is necessary for the child's healthy emotional and personality development; such an attachment is a prerequisite for a maturing child to have healthy, secondary attachment relationships as the child's social world expands. Attachment theory and research indicate that attachment relationships are demonstrated in clearly observable attachment behaviors (Ainsworth & Wittig, 1969; Bowlby, 1969).

Parent-child attachment relationships may be healthy or unhealthy. Healthy attachment relationships develop when the parent or caregiver adequately fulfills the needs of the child; unhealthy attachment relationships develop when these needs are not fulfilled on a consistent basis. Children have three basic needs that transcend developmental levels and each child's unique history. These are the need for nurturance, the need for stimulation, and the need for protection.

Nurturance includes both physical and emotional nurturance. Physical nurturance refers to being assured of adequate food, sleep, good hygiene, and medical and dental care. Emotional nurturance is a prerequisite to self-esteem and includes being valued, loved, cared for, and listened to by persons upon whom the child relies for care.

Stimulation includes both social company and involvement in play and exploratory activities that facilitate cognitive, social, and physical development. Initially, parents are the primary mediators of the world for the child, and they themselves meet the child's need for company through playing, talking, and holding. As the child develops, the circle of friends gradually increases from siblings, close family friends, and relatives to include peers, teachers, and other adults outside the family.

Children need assurance of safety in their environment, and rely on parents or parent-figures to protect and buffer them from abuse from persons and from dangers in the physical environment. They need consistent and predictable limits that can give them freedom to explore and to express themselves in ways that are not harmful to themselves or to others.

As the child develops, the content of what parents should provide in each of these areas changes, yet there is continuity with the child always needing assurance of nurturance, stimulation, and protection as he or she faces each new developmental task.

In evaluating whether the child's current needs are being met, one needs to look at the child's present needs both developmentally and in relation to the child's history. Assessment of the degree to which each of these needs is being fulfilled is most accurate when behavioral observations of the child with the parents are integrated with information obtained in clinical interviews of the parents about their experiences with the child.

The parents' own histories of attachment and parental care influence their relationships with their children (Main & Goldwyn, 1984; Steele, 1970, 1980, 1983). Parents who themselves received empathic care from their parents tend to provide empathic care for their children and to develop healthy attachment relationships with them (Kohut, 1977; Steele, 1983). The child who experiences empathic parental care develops a secure, healthy attachment relationship with the parents and a healthy, coherent sense of self.

Unhealthy attachment relationships develop when parents who had poor attachments with their parents are unable to develop healthy relationships with their children and to provide empathic care. Steele (1983) describes how the cycle of inadequate parental care is repeated from generation to generation:

> Because of deprivation in her own early life, a mother is unable to fully attach to her new baby. In the absence of good attachment, she cannot provide adequate empathic care. She thus brings up an emotionally deprived baby who will grow up to be a parent who attaches poorly and cannot provide empathic care, and so the cycle tends to repeat from generation to generation. (p. 235)

When parents are unable to respond appropriately to their child's needs, an integrated sense of self does not develop. Steele (1983) explains:

> If (parental) responses to the infant's needs are not reliably and repeatedly appropriate, the infant's inner sensations are not validated or integrated, and an integrated sense of self does not develop...the infant remains persistently oriented toward the outside world for cues and guidance, disregarding to a greater or lesser extent its own internal sensations, needs, and wishes. The subsequent diminished,

often tragically low self-esteem is a characteristic which we see throughout life into adulthood. (p. 241)

There are two basic forms of unhealthy attachment relationships: an "anxious-avoidant" (or "unattached") pattern and an "anxious-resistant" (or "insecure") pattern (Ainsworth & Wittig, 1969; Bowlby, 1988; Egeland & Sroufe, 1981). An anxious-avoidant attachment pattern develops when a parent expresses rejecting attitudes and behaviors toward the child and is emotionally unavailable to meet the child's needs for nurturance and attention. An anxious-resistant attachment pattern develops when a parent confuses his or her emotional, and sometimes sexual, needs with those of the child and uses the child to satisfy those needs. In an anxious-resistant relationship, the child's needs are not met on a consistent basis. However, the child, yearning for closeness and approval of the parent, may learn to accept whatever parental attention is available (including sexualized attention) (see Haynes-Seman & Krugman, 1989), although it is not healthy for the child. Each of these two basic forms of unhealthy attachment relationships can be identified by a different set of observable behaviors in the relationship.

The child's behavior in interactions with the parents are legitimate indices to the broader experiences that have given rise to these behavioral patterns. Observation of behavior provides a window into experiences that are not always available in words. Kohut (1977) describes the value of observations in the psychoanalytic situation and the need for broader application of what is learned from observation:

Yet I cannot help but maintain that the access to the significance of the experiential world of man, and thus to the significance of behavior, that is opened to us by the observation of...deeply rooted phenomena in the psychoanalytic situation is unequaled and that the conclusions to which

we come on the basis of these observations deserve indeed
to be applied broadly. (pp. 115–116)

When one observes the child with the parent, the observer is
viewing the history of the child's relationship with that parent.
For this reason, one or two episodes from the child's interactions with the parent illustrate the kinds of day-to-day experiences that have led to the more general pattern. Stechler and
Halton (1987) speak to this issue:

> The selection of one or two episodes from each family to-
> gether with a summary of the characteristic developmental
> pattern does not imply that the events of the selected epi-
> sodes have produced the general pattern. You are asked to
> envision a multitudinous repetition of similar episodes, each
> unique, but qualitatively similar, that has created the gen-
> eral configuration. (pp. 829–830)

PARENT-CHILD SEXUAL ABUSE AS A DISORDER OF ATTACHMENT

Parent-child sex abuse is a disorder of attachment; it can occur
only in an unhealthy attachment relationship. Because an unhealthy attachment relationship can be directly observed, even
if the actual abuse cannot, one may conduct an assessment analysis that first identifies and appropriately eliminates healthy attachment relationships as suspect for sex abuse and then exam-
ines unhealthy attachments for specific indicators of abuse. If
abuse has occurred in an unhealthy attachment relationship,
there will be unmistakable behavioral and clinical indicators.

Dysfunctional parent-child relationships develop when parents fail to maintain generational boundaries and to fulfill their
parental roles with their children. These dysfunctional patterns
may or may not be manifested in parent-child sexual abuse. Lidz

(1968) describes the distorted patterns that emerge when parents rely on their children to meet their needs:

> The parents are the guiding, nurturing, teaching generation who must give of themselves so that the children can grow. They may be dependent upon one another but should not be dependent upon immature children. The children must be dependent on parental figures and be free to invest their energies in their own development. While a sexual relationship between the parents is not only permitted, but expected, all overt sexual behaviors between a child and other members of the family is prohibited, which helps assure the child will seek fulfillment outside the family. Parents can inappropriately break the generation boundaries in a number of ways; for example, by utilizing a child to fill needs unsatisfied by the spouse; by a mother's failing to establish boundaries between herself and a son whom she expects to live out the life closed to her because she is a woman; by a father's behaving more like a child than a spouse and offering his wife little except satisfaction of her needs to mother. (p. 59)

Unhealthy parent-child relationships such as those described by Lidz are observable. This includes sexually abusive relationships. Both the child's behaviors and the abusive parent's behaviors, in interaction with each other and separately, provide clues to the inappropriate nature of their relationship.

FACTORS THAT LEAD TO AND MAINTAIN INCESTUOUS RELATIONSHIPS

The generational repetition of unhealthy attachment relationships is a factor that makes the attachment context particularly useful in determining whether abuse has occurred and, if it has, in identifying the etiology of this particular form of disturbed attachment relations within the family. Clinicians have proposed various explanations for the development of incestuous relationships within a family.

Gaddini (1983) describes sexual abuse as a search for intimacy and physical closeness:

At the basis of perpetrating what society rightly considers a crime, there is a quest for intimacy and for physical contact, which both partners, the perpetrator no less than the child like every human being, is entitled to receive in early life, and of which, in the case of incest, they have been deprived. (p. 358)

Steele (1991) contends that the "universal wish for company" may be at the root of incestuous relationships:

From earliest infancy there seems to be a basic need....Anna Freud described it as the infant's "wish for company," existing along with the basic needs for food, sleep, and protection that are satisfied by the primary attachment figure, usually the mother....This "wish for company" remains with us all of our lives....If the mother has not been adequately there, the need and yearning for that kind of care persists, and the process of separation remains difficult and incomplete. Although physical and hormonal sexual development have matured, the sexual behavior in the incest participant is still deeply determined by the yearning for what is basically primary maternal care....Many incest participants, both adult and child, speak of emptiness, lack of satisfaction, and a yearning for closeness, care, and attention. (pp. 31–32)

In the incestuous relationship, the abusive parent may be trying to recreate with the child the closeness with a maternal figure that cannot be relinquished or to create closeness that was never experienced with the maternal figure in infancy (Steele, 1991):

> The continued need for... (an incestuous) relationship may arise from deprivation of adequate care in early development, or just the opposite, it may result from perpetuation of close maternal care and involvement that cannot be relinquished. (p. 17)

Conceptualization of the incestuous relationship as an attempt to fill the void left when each participant has been deprived of normal affection and closeness in other relationships does not remove the responsibility from the abusive parent. As Steele (1991) points out, the adult and not the child is the one who breaks the incest barrier:

> ...could the incest barrier be broken without the cooperation or coercion of the adult? It seems unlikely that a reasonably normal adult could not resist even the most seductive sexual advances of a child. (p. 31)

Incestuous patterns may continue across generations as parents who grew up in incestuous families recreate their experiences in a new family. This repetition may be different depending on the sex of the victim and perpetrator and on whether the parent identifies with the perpetrator or with the nonprotective parent.

A mother victimized by her father or stepfather may identify with her mother and fail to protect her child from sexual abuse by an adult partner as her mother failed to protect her; or she may project her experiences of abuse by a father or father-figure onto current relationships and mistakenly believe that her child is being abused by father as she was abused by her father as a child.

A father abused by a parent or a person in a position of trust may identify with the abuser and repeat the pattern of abuse with his son or daughter. In incestuous families, the parents' ambivalent or conflicted feelings about their own sexual experiences with a parent or parent-figure may lead them to conclude that this is not harmful to the child or that the child is seeking this form of intimacy with them.

From this perspective, parent-child sexual abuse is not the problem. It is the attempt to solve the problem. Only by identifying the problems that the parents are trying to resolve, can one provide effective treatment for parents and the child. Understanding of the problem requires that one examine all the relationships within the family. This examination makes available to the evaluator family dynamics and relationships that allowed a child to be abused or led to a parent's mistaken belief that the other parent was abusing the child. This mistaken belief may have led to separation and divorce or may have followed separation and divorce. A custody battle may or may not be in progress at the time of the allegations.

Healing involves all members of the family whether abuse occurred or not. This healing can begin only after the problem that led to the abuse or to the mistaken belief is accurately diagnosed.

DYNAMICS AND RELATIONSHIPS IN INCESTUOUS FAMILIES

The dynamics that lead to and maintain the child within an incestuous relationship with a parent or parent-figure indicate the need for assessing the child within the context of the family and family relationships. The *secret* can be maintained even into adulthood by persons sexually abused by parents or parent-figures when they were children (Berliner & Conte, 1993; Finkelhor, Hotaling, Lewis, & Smith, 1990; Summit, 1983). Steele (1991) suggests that the relative neglect of incest in treatment of adult patients may be related to

> ...a tendency of incest participants to consciously avoid revealing their experiences or unconsciously repress and deny them out of shame and fear of disapproval. Because incest victims have a low self-esteem and distrust of people, they do not often seek...therapy, and their characteristic defenses and adaptations make it extremely difficult for them to take part...in a (therapeutic) situation. (p.16)

In familial sexual abuse, the child is in a relationship of dependency with the abuser and with disclosure risks loss of the only family he or she has. As Summit (1983) points out, children may be pressured to recant by the reaction of other family members. Children who disclose often face difficulties in being believed or in receiving support from the other parent. This occurs primarily in intact families in which the nonabusive parent is in a couple relationship with the abusive adult. The disclosing child may also face rejection by siblings who blame this child for destroying the family. Summit (1983) conceptualizes the child's failure to disclose or subsequent recantation as an *accommodation syndrome*. For the child, keeping the abuse secret is a "source of fear" but also a "promise of safety."

Finkelhor and Browne (1985) describe four traumagenic states specific to parent-child sexual abuse: traumatic sexualization, betrayal, powerlessness, and stigmatization. These states explain the process through which the child is drawn into and maintained within a sexually abusive relationship with a parent or parent-figure.

A child involved in sexual games and activities from early infancy and long before he or she knows right from wrong may experience *traumatic sexualization.* Such a child may "emerge with inappropriate repertoires of sexual behavior, confusion or misconceptions about sexual self concepts, and unusual emotional associations to sexual activities" (Finkelhor & Brown, 1985, p. 531).

When sexual abuse begins at an early age, the child may initially perceive the sexualization as attention and interest from the parent. Later the child feels betrayed by the abusive parent upon learning that the sexual activities are harmful and frowned upon by others; however, powerlessness and stigmatization maintain the child within the sexually abusive relationship and ensure secrecy. The child is powerless to stop the abuse, and the child's dependency on and affection for the abusive parent often trap the child in the abusive relationship. The child keeps the secret because of fear that peers and family members will stigmatize him or her for being an incest participant.

The child may have conflicted feelings about a sexually abusing parent or parent-figure and may wish for a relationship with that person uncontaminated by abuse. Well-intentioned efforts to protect the child from any contact with the alleged perpetrator may prevent the child from confronting his or her feelings about the abuse and the abuser. Furchner (1989) addresses this issue:

> How well do we have under control our own anger or punitive responses toward the perpetrator? Because if you get really angry with the perpetrator like the child is mad at the father, then that child is not going to be able to tell you the other half of that feeling that is how much the child loves the father and how much he or she misses him. (p. 11)

The child may feel guilty for being involved in the abuse and may believe the evaluator is directing angry feelings for the abusive parent toward him or her. James (1989) elaborates:

> Abused children learn to "read" adults quickly. They often interpret the therapist's hatred of the perpetrator as directed toward themselves, since they secretly know the abuse was their fault. Believing (or realizing) that the therapist hates the person they love and upon whom they are emotionally and physically dependent leads to feelings of guilt and shame in the child, and creates a chasm between the child and the therapist. (p. 18)

Sexual abuse differs from other forms of maltreatment in that there are reinforcers not present in emotionally or physically abusive parent-child relationships. The child may feel guilty because he or she enjoyed the abuse or the benefits derived from it. James (1989) writes:

> With sexual abuse, the child may initially experience physical excitement and the satisfaction of a reward, or may experience heightened stature as a result of sharing a secret with an adult. At later developmental stages, he may experience guilt feelings for having enjoyed, or at least not having resisted the experience. He may feel shame, believing himself responsible for causing the removal of a parent from the home. He may later long for the abusive parent; have feelings of shame and stigmatization; believe he is gay, gross, perverted, or that his only value is as a sexual object; or he may fear that he will be found out, or that he will abuse others. (p. 6)

Rarely are disclosures made in a clear, direct statement to the nonabusive parent or to someone outside the family. Young children who do not recognize that the activities are inappropriate are likely to disclose the abuse "accidentally" rather than "directly" (Sorensen & Snow, 1991). Accidental disclosures include unusual statements or behaviors that lead the parent or someone else to suspect the child is being abused.

Older children who understand the consequences of disclosure give clues to abusive experiences through stories, metaphors, and drawings. They may fear they will not be believed or that disclosure will lead to negative consequences for themselves or someone they love.

CONCLUSION

An accusation or actual conduct of parent-child sexual abuse occurs within a family. All relationships within the family are affected by the sexual abuse or by the belief that it occurred. Examination of the attachment relationships among the family members provides an evaluator access to significant information not otherwise available.

Such an examination permits inclusion of all members of the family, including the children whether they are verbal or not, and gives value to each of their contributions, behavioral and clinical. Because healthy and unhealthy attachment relationships can be identified and distinguished by observable attachment behaviors and clinical information, one can eliminate from suspicion healthy attachment relationships, in which sexual abuse cannot exist, and examine unhealthy attachment relationships for specific behavioral and clinical indicators of sexual abuse.

The Kempe Interactional Assessment for Parent-Child Sexual Abuse, by assessing attachment relationships through examination of family attachment behaviors and clinical information, makes most beneficial use of the family dynamics and fosters professional consideration of all available information.

2

Design for a Complete and Objective Process: How to Get All the Information You Need

The accuracy and value of an assessment procedure depends on the completeness of the information gathered and the discrimination with which the information is evaluated. The Kempe Interactional Assessment for Parent-Child Sexual Abuse is a procedure that gathers information from readily available sources, makes available information from traditionally overlooked sources, and provides for the strengths and weaknesses of its investigative components. Interactional assessment, by definition and by design, is a process of true inquiry, full analysis, and objective determination. It is *not* a process to validate a preconception centered around a hunch that sexual abuse has taken place or did not occur.

The Kempe Interactional Assessment for Parent-Child Sexual Abuse is designed and conducted to produce interactions among all family members and to encourage the children to express themselves in their own language throughout the assessment. Integral to the process is the fact that children, verbal or not, can and will communicate if given the opportunity; interactional assessment makes directly available to the evaluator the child's experiences with each parent and with significant others through observable patterns of behavior. Parents, through interactions and recall of significant childhood experiences, also communicate the quality and content of their family relationships. The evaluator is attentive to the communications of all family members and gives each member sure affirmation that they are being understood. All children in the family are included in the assessment even though the allegations may directly involve only one of them.

INTERACTIONAL ASSESSMENT IN THE CONTEXT OF CURRENT GUIDELINES

Currently there is no consensus among professionals about the most effective methods for evaluation of allegations of parent-child sexual abuse. However, the Kempe Interactional Assessment draws on the strengths of each of the existing guidelines for clinical evaluation of allegations of parent-child sexual abuse that are available from the American Professional Society on the Abuse of Children (APSAC) (1990) and the American Academy of Child and Adolescent Psychiatry (AACAP) (1990) and provides an opportunity for future consensus based upon specific training, experience, and conduct.

The Setting

The setting in which the evaluations are conducted is of paramount importance. Family sessions must be conducted in a room that promotes free, but fully observable, interactions among the family members. The environment should be comfortable, permit relaxation, and be obviously safe to each of the participants, particularly the children. The entry door should be visible to those in the room.

The room should be furnished with couches and chairs for adults as well as small chairs and tables for children. The parents and children should have a sense of privacy in the session, except for the presence of the evaluator. Videotaping equipment, except for discreetly placed microphones, should be set up in an adjoining room to minimize distraction but with a full range of view. The room should be arranged to provide a face-on view of evaluation participants to the video cameras.

Evaluation Tools and Materials

The APSAC and AACAP guidelines recognize that play materials may help the child communicate what may have happened to him or her. The APSAC guidelines view these "nonverbal tools" as assisting the child's communication. The AACAP Guidelines suggest that anatomically correct dolls or drawings may be helpful in assessing child sexual abuse. They caution that it is not necessary to use anatomically correct dolls, but they indicate that the dolls may help children demonstrate what happened in the event that they cannot tell or draw what happened.

In the interactional assessment, play materials, easily accessible to the child throughout the assessment, have a much greater role than demonstrative reenactment. They are a medium through which the child can express a whole range of conscious and unconscious feelings and project his or her own experiences into the external world.

Play materials should be appropriate to the child's developmental level, maintain the child's interest, and provide a ready vehicle for the child to communicate feelings and experiences with important persons in his or her life. Plastic materials such as paper, crayons, magic markers, scissors, and Play Doh help the child to say what he cannot say in words. Puzzles and books not only provide opportunity for engagement or disengagement with the parents, but also may be used to communicate the child's experiences with or feelings toward each parent. For example, the book the child chooses to share with each parent may show the child's different feelings toward each in response to the current situation.

Symbolic play materials help the child to explore feelings and experiences or to reenact or even gain control over past trauma. Materials that encourage symbolic play include wood building blocks, trucks and cars; aggressive and nonaggressive animals; dolls, blankets, doll clothes, bottles, baby carrier, bassinet, tea set, and telephones; doll house with furniture and doll figures; aggressive and nonaggressive animal hand puppets.

The evaluator may wish to have additional materials available during the play interview with the child. These might include anatomically correct dolls, medical kit, line drawings of front and back view of a nude boy and girl, and projective test materials.

Observing the Child with Each Parent

APSAC guidelines suggest that observation of the child with each parent may be useful in providing information about the "overall quality of the relationship" (p. 4). The AACAP guidelines indicate that it is useful to observe the child with each parent in certain cases in which the allegations are more likely to be mistaken or false with respect to the accused parent. Both sets of guidelines assume that information available from observing the child with each parent is limited.

In the interactional assessment, observation of the child with each parent in different interactive contexts is an essential part of the information to be considered in determining whether the allegations are valid or mistaken with respect to the accused parent. The actual occurrence of abuse or the mistaken belief that abuse was inflicted when it never occurred are symptoms of an attachment disorder that has its roots in the parents' own relationships with their parents.

According to Steele (1983), observing the child with each parent not only provides information about the child's experiences, but also gives access to the parent's own childhood experiences:

> In the maltreatment situation, we believe we can see in the parent-infant interaction the experiences that instigate in the infant the psychological patterns that produce the behavior of the very adult we are simultaneously observing. Thus, in this "experiment of nature" we are seeing a much foreshortened longitudinal study. We observe in a single scenario the infantile beginning and the adult outcome without having to do twenty-year-long follow up studies. To be sure, many other things have entered into the adult's psychic development and modified it, but the threads of continuity in psychic function between the infant and the adult are astonishingly clear. (pp. 235–236)

Observing the child with each parent provides a check on the accuracy of the parents' reports of their experiences with the child. The child's presence during the interview also makes accessible to the evaluator the kinds of experiences the parent had as a child and the manner in which these are influencing the parent's current behavior toward the child (Fraiberg, 1980) or toward the spouse or ex-spouse. The main tenet of the Kempe Interactional Assessment is that the child's experiences with each parent can be made accessible through a protocol that combines observation of parent-child interactions with the clinical interview of the parents and the play interview with the child.

The quality of the relationship is directly related to the child's experiences with each parent. Assessment of the quality of the relationship by definition includes information about the child's experiences with the attachment figure that have led to the development of the attachment pattern observed. This includes both information available in the interview with the parents and in the observation of parent-child interactions.

Just as the child's attachment pattern cannot be assessed on the basis of the child's behavior in one situation (such as separation or reunion), it would be inappropriate to draw conclusions about whether abuse has or has not occurred based on a single episode of behavior, such as the child's initial reaction to the accused parent or parent-figure. A pattern of behaviors in different contexts that occur routinely during a day combined with clinical data provide the information that allows the evaluator to assess the nature of the child's experiences with each parent, including but not limited to involvement in inappropriate sexual activities.

Observation Protocol

Because the APSAC and AACAP guidelines ascribe limited usefulness to what can be learned from observing the child with each parent, they do not describe the kinds of interactive situations in which observations should be made. Other clinicians have used observations of the child's interactions with the accused parent as part of the assessment data; however, to our knowledge these observations have not been videotaped and there was no systematic protocol that provided a wide range of situations in which observations were made (Benedek & Schetky,

1985; Green, 1986; Kaplan & Kaplan, 1981). In contrast, the Kempe Interactional Assessment provides a systematic approach to the use of observed parent-child interactions and relies on observation-derived information as essential in determining whether abuse has occurred.

The interactive contexts are designed to incorporate the kinds of situations children and parents encounter routinely during a day. As with the attachment situations in Ainsworth's Strange Situation Paradigm (Ainsworth & Wittig, 1969), which were designed to elicit attachment behaviors of infants at one year of age, the situations included in the Kempe Interactional Assessment are designed to facilitate a wide range of parent-child interactions, to permit observation of significant attachment behaviors between children and parents, and to permit assessment of the degree to which the parent appropriately meets the child's needs for nurturance, stimulation, and protection.

The situations are designed to help the child participate behaviorally and, if possible, verbally, throughout the session. These standard situations include a time when the parents are alone, reunion of the children with their parents, unstructured play among the family prior to the clinical interview of the parents, the child's presence and play during the clinical interview, a snack shared by parents and children, and separation of parents and children. When the parents are divorced, a transition between the noncustodial and custodial parent may also be videotaped.

Parents are encouraged to perform routine caregiving activities such as diaper changing, feeding, and setting limits as needed throughout the session. Parents and children take breaks as needed during the session.

Interactions between the parents when they are alone waiting for the children to join them provide information about the couple relationship and about the anxiety of each about the session. The parents may engage in unusual behaviors with toys that give clues to their own childhood issues that are impacting current relationships or to their activities with the child that they hope to keep secret.

Observations during reunion capture the time when both parents and children may be most anxious about seeing each other. The child's behaviors at reunion often bring into sharp focus the child's experiences with the parent and how he or she interprets any current prohibitions that may exist that preclude contact with the parent(s). In healthy relationships, children are observably happy to see loved ones they have not seen, but this may not be observed when sexual abuse has occurred or when the relationship has been disrupted by the mistaken allegation of sexual abuse.

If abuse has occurred, the child will give subtle signs of anxiety that might be missed without review of videotape. If the child has been drawn into making false statements, the child's anxiety will be expressed differently and will resolve as the child realizes the parent is the good and protective parent that he or she knows. The source of this anxiety may not be apparent immediately but can be determined based on behaviors and words during the entire session. The parent's behavior toward the child in this initial period may give meaning to the parent's behavior with the toys or show unsuccessful efforts to control behaviors that he or she believes others would interpret as inappropriate.

The initial unstructured play period prior to the interview provides an opportunity for parents and children to become comfortable with each other and with the room. Of particular significance is how the family uses the time to catch up on what each member has been doing during any separation, to share past experiences, or to discuss what the children perceive as having led to the current problem in the family. When the children are alone with the parents, the children themselves demonstrate protection issues by controlling distance or closeness, making or avoiding eye contact, or giving other signs of comfort or anxiety.

To help promote interactions between parents and children, the evaluator encourages the parents to help the children feel comfortable and to settle in. Even though the parents may be aware of the camera, familiar patterns of behavior emerge as the child responds as he or she normally would and the parent responds to the child's words and behaviors.

Patterns of interaction and behaviors during the initial play period may be contrasted with patterns observed later during the clinical interview, when the parents must divide attention between the children and the evaluator. During the clinical interview, the parents may experience increased stress related to the questions or to the child's behavior. When the parents are distracted by the interview, the child has the opportunity to control distance or proximity, engagement or disengagement. The child's verbal and nonverbal behavior in the context of the parents' responses to questions may also be informative about the child's experiences with each parent.

The parent's attentiveness to the child during the clinical interview may be contrasted with the attentiveness during other assessment components. Snack occurs about midway in the session. This provides another opportunity for parents and children to be observed together without the distraction of the evaluator or the interview questions.

If the parents and children have been separated and then reunited for the assessment, it is informative whether or not they enjoy this potentially nurturing snack time together. This also provides a brief recess for the parents and children from the interview. Most families eat together routinely. During this familiar activity, parents and children relate to each other as they normally do during meals; patterns that have developed around mealtime may be observed. Interactions during this time often reveal the perceptions of each member of the family of other family members and the experiences that have led to healthy or unhealthy attachment relationships within the family.

Observation of the separation of parents and child at the end of the parent-child session is particularly significant for its emotional content and the behaviors of those who remain in the room after the separation. If the children are in foster care, they leave the parents to return to foster parents because it is easier to leave than to be left, and it is also easier to leave if they can be assured that someone will be there to care for them.

In cases where custody is not being exercised equally, the children may remain in the room while the noncustodial parent leaves and then have a reunion with the custodial parent. In the assessment, a contrast can be made between the children's account to the custodial parent of their previous assessment activities and the actual videotaped record.

The Child's Presence During the Clinical Interview

The AACAP guidelines (1990) emphasize the importance of evaluating the child within the context of the family and the danger of drawing conclusions based on inadequate information:

> ...evaluators often use inadequate diagnostic techniques or fail to evaluate the child within the context of the family. If conclusions are drawn on the basis of inadequate or insufficient information, children may be harmed, parent-child relationships seriously damaged, and these cases contaminated to the point that courts and other professionals have great difficulty sorting out what did or did not occur. (p. 1)

Interactional assessment builds upon this concept by making the presence of the child during the clinical interviews of the parents an integral component of the assessment. The child may then participate and react, verbally and through behavior, as information about the family in which he or she lives is gathered.

The parents' feelings and attitudes that may be expressed in words during the interview have been experienced on a daily basis by the child through the parents' behaviors and words to the child. Parents who show a lack of awareness of boundaries in what they discuss in front of the child also show this same lack of boundaries in their day-to-day relationship with the child.

This is not a new experience for the child. An assumption can be made that whatever is discussed in the interview has been a part of the child's experience. If parents express negative feelings about the child, an ex-spouse, or their childhood experiences, it can be assumed that the child has not previously been protected from these feelings. The child will have experienced negative feelings about self or others or problems related to drug and alcohol use in the parents' attitudes and behaviors outside of the evaluation context.

Parents who respond to questions about concerns that brought them to the evaluation are presumably relating the child's actual experiences as reported to them by the child or displayed in observable behaviors. The parents' report of experiences and behaviors during the assessment do not change the child's actual experiences and may even strengthen his or her need to communicate that experience to others in whatever way he or she can (Sorensen & Snow, 1991).

Often it is the parents' responses to questions that seem to trigger the child's memories of actual experiences. As the child demonstrates behaviorally or in words what has happened, the parents' responses to interview questions provide information that gives meaning to the child's behavior and words.

An evaluator must be aware that if abuse did occur, the child may be exposed to past trauma by being with the parent during the clinical interview. Having this experience may be necessary to help the child recall and put behind him the past trauma. This is an accepted part of what a therapist does. Play therapist James (1989) writes:

> The therapist must often reopen doors to terrible places in order to help the child work the trauma through, and in so doing, he exposes himself to the stories and descriptions of the events. And yet if he responds, overtly or subtly, with his own feelings of horror, the child and his caregivers are given the messages that even inured professionals cannot face the enormity of the trauma the child has suffered. (pp. xi–xii)

The child's presence during the clinical interview is healthy for the child. If abuse occurred, the session with the abusive parent serves as a catharsis for the child. The child's behavior or words reveal that the child is not only trying to tell others but also the abuser that he or she knows what happened. By revealing the abuse, he or she is seeking protection from being hurt again. The child who is present during the interview with each parent learns that the evaluator wants to know what happened in the family; the child has the opportunity to listen to each parent without having to challenge what they say. The child is present with both parents together in an intact family and with each parent separately in the case of a family in which the parents are divorced.

The message to the child is that the evaluator listens, wants to understand, and will protect him or her. If no abuse occurred or the child was abused by someone else, the child has an opportunity to express him or herself and have these experiences validated. Misinterpretations may be corrected when information from many sources is utilized in the evaluation process.

Parental Interview Protocol

The APSAC guidelines (1990) indicate that "it is not necessary to interview the accused or suspected individual in order to form an opinion about possible sexual abuse of the child" (p. 3). When the accused is a parent, however, APSAC guidelines suggest it is "preferred practice...for the child evaluator to contact or interview the parent" (p. 3). The AACAP guidelines indicate the need to obtain a history from each parent, especially when the allegations arise during a custody dispute in divorce.

The Kempe Interactional Assessment considers that a clinical interview with each parent provides an essential opportunity to obtain vital information from each available source. The interview questions are open-ended and allow the evaluator to probe topics that are brought up by the parents as appropriate.

This interview differs from the traditional history-taking interview in that its focus is on relationships, feelings, perceptions, and experiences rather than on a time-line development. The interview topics are designed to cast a wide net. That is, not every question will get a probative answer. Inquiring about a wide spectrum of experiences across the life span of the individual provides the opportunity for things to come out rather than demanding discrete information. Because each case is in a sense unique, the evaluator does not know what is critical in a particular case until all the data are collected.

The interview is not conducted like a test with right and wrong answers. It is conducted as a conversation designed to elicit the parents' perspective about their current situation and life experiences leading up to the current situation.

Many clinicians are uncomfortable with the idea of asking parents what they consider to be intimate or private details about their life experiences while the children are present. That discomfort may be alleviated by learning to frame and focus the questions in a particular way.

In the Kempe Interactional Assessment for Parent-Child Sexual Abuse, the questions are designed and framed to explore family relationships and experiences—experiences that are a part of the child's life because they have impacted in a very real way the parent's attitudes and behaviors toward the child even prior to the child's birth. An overview of the topics explored with the parents may be useful in illustrating the kinds of information that are available from the clinical interview with the parents.

The interview begins with a discussion of what brought the family to this evaluation and invariably deals with the allegations that led to the evaluation. The child's behavior as the parents talk is an important part of the information. This is true whether the perpetrator is denying the abuse or whether the parent is reporting valid or false experiences for the child.

The evaluator explores with each parent their concerns or the concerns of others about their child. Each parent's response provides clues about what led to the concerns that something happened to the child and why one parent or others may believe the other parent sexually abused the child. The evaluator will follow up any issues that may come up in what the parent is saying about the situation or about their relationship with the other parent. In a divorce case, the evaluator should inquire about the involvement of the noncustodial parent with the child prior to and subsequent to the allegations of sexual abuse.

The evaluator may inquire about specific allegations in more detail later when the child is not present. An accused parent's denial or an accusing parent's belief that abuse has occurred is not the criterion for determining whether the allegations are valid or mistaken. Each parent's statements about the alleged abuse during the clinical interview are only part of the total data that will enable the evaluation team to draw a conclusion about what may or may not have happened to the child.

Questions about the parent's experiences with the child focus on transition points in the parent-child relationship. Open-ended questions explore each parent's perception of and experiences with each child. Although the evaluator may begin with the pregnancy with the oldest child, it is important to determine whether there were previous or intervening pregnancies and what happened with each. The evaluator explores with each parent their experiences related to the pregnancy, birth, delivery, first reaction to each child, and early experiences with each in terms of caregiving and social activities and their perception of the responsiveness of each child to parenting efforts.

The evaluator then turns to the current relationship with each child. Questions explore the parent's perception of each child, involvement in day-to-day care of the child, hard and easy aspects of parenting, limit setting and discipline methods, and the anticipated outcome of their parenting efforts with regard to their children's future lives.

The length of time required to complete this portion of the interview varies. Ideally the evaluator finishes this portion of the interview in about an hour. The shift in focus from the history with the child to childhood history of the parent, the couple relationship, and other life-style issues provides an appropriate time to break for a snack. The evaluator, however, should be sensitive to the child's well-being and break for a snack when it seems appropriate.

After the snack, the evaluator explores with each parent memories of childhood including experiences of being cared for by parents, sibling relationships, and relationships with significant others. Information provided at any point during the interview may provide understanding of the parent's own childhood experiences as this gives insight into unresolved issues that are influencing present relationships. The parents are asked about significant losses or separations in their lives.

To gain an understanding of other factors that may influence current relationships, the evaluator asks probative questions about alcohol and drug use, both past and present. Although it is not expected that parents will be completely forthcoming about this, they provide enough information to determine whether a more complete substance abuse evaluation is needed. The consistency or lack of consistency between each parent's report of their use and that of the other parent also provides additional information about whether this problem needs to be further evaluated.

Previous relationships provide a context for understanding of the couple relationship in an intact family or in separation or divorce. This may be explored in terms of dating, previous marriages, and other significant relationships prior to the parents' relationship with each other.

The evaluator explores each parent's perception of and experiences with the other parent (or partner) through probative questions about first attraction, positive and negative aspects of the relationship, and current problems facing the couple or individuals. Although the questions do not explicitly inquire about sexual satisfaction, the information shared by each parent allows the evaluator to assess the sexual satisfaction and, in some cases, the sexual orientation or preference of each parent. If a parent wishes to give a more detailed account of the sexual relationship that would not be appropriate for the child to hear, he or she may request a time alone to share this information.

The evaluator ends the interview by allowing each parent to consider their life history and explore changes they would choose in that history. Their responses to this inquiry provide insight into what each parent perceives as influencing the current problem and what might have led to a different outcome. They may focus on past trauma that has led them to the present situation, or on the present situation and what they might have done to prevent it or how they hope to resolve the current problem.

Play Interview with the Child

An important component of the Kempe Interactional Assessment is the individual child play interview (Jones & McQuiston, 1986). The interview provides a unique and essential opportunity for the child to express his or her feelings and to demonstrate his or her experiences through play materials. A properly trained and skilled evaluator who is attentive to and understanding of the child's behavior, symbolic play themes, drawings, affective expression, spontaneous statements or statements in response to directed questions when available may conduct a highly informative conversational interview with the child. Information obtained in the family session provides an essential context for understanding the meaning of the child's words and behaviors during the play interview.

Psychiatric Evaluation of the Parents

When information obtained in the clinical interview raises questions about a psychiatric contribution to a disturbed parent-child relationship, a complete psychiatric evaluation of each parent is indicated. The evaluation should include psychological tests and, in some cases, sex-offender specific examinations. In addition to these tests, a psychiatric interview that includes a detailed sexual history may be needed to assess the nature and severity of the psychiatric disturbance or sexual deviancy. The parents' psychiatric diagnosis may or may not affect their parenting capacity and explain their sexual deviance.

Many parents who sexually abuse their children have no psychiatric diagnosis. Steele (1991) speaks to misconceptions about parents who break the incest barrier:

> Recent voluminous literature on child abuse has shown that consummate incest is a fairly common occurrence in our own culture as well as worldwide, and there is no reason to believe it has not always been so. As far as the taboo is concerned, it seems to have applied more to recognition and talking about incest rather than to incest itself. The general public and many psychiatrists and psychoanalysts still find it difficult to believe that the barrier is broken except by psychotic or unusually depraved people. (p. 16)

Persons deprived of love and maternal care in their earliest years or who were themselves, in the words of Steele, *incest participants* may break the incest barrier in an attempt to satisfy what Steele (1991) describes as a "yearning for closeness, care, and attention" (p. 32).

A Team Approach

The APSAC and AACAP guidelines consider it essential that evaluators of child sexual abuse have expertise in child sexual abuse or have certain clinical credentials respectively. Both guidelines suggest that a team approach may be useful in some cases, although it is not essential.

The Kempe Interactional Assessment also emphasizes the importance of a team approach in addition to individual evaluator expertise in child sexual abuse, knowledge of attachment theory, and clinical skills in interview and observation. The team should consist of clinicians from at least two different disciplines, including developmental or clinical psychology, clinical social work, psychiatric nursing, child or adult psychiatry, and have available for consultation clinicians with extensive experience in evaluation and treatment of children and families as well as attorneys whose practice involves representation of parents and children in these cases.

The team should have available for review the video and written transcripts of the parent-child sessions, the clinical interviews, the play interviews with the child and siblings, and information from other sources, including child protection team, social services, and police reports.

Review of videotaped records of each session by a clinical team is essential for accurate interpretation of the interviews, observations, and other materials. This team process minimizes the opportunities for a mistaken focus or interpretation. An evaluation report drafted or reviewed by the team can delineate multidisciplined, clinical findings that support or refute the allegations and indicate issues that need to be addressed in treatment for child and family.

CONCLUSION

The Kempe Interactional Assessment for Parent-Child Sexual Abuse provides information about family dynamics and relationships that would not be available without the clinical interview with each parent with the child present, observation of the child with each parent, and play interview with the child. The synergism of information obtained from parents, siblings, and the alleged child-victim allows the team to draw definitive conclusions about whether abuse occurred.

Validation of the abuse does not depend on the verbal disclosure of the child, confession of the perpetrator, or the convic-

tion of the other parent that abuse has occurred. It depends on
gathering and sifting through information from multiple sources.

3

Evaluation Tasks, Skills, and Pitfalls

The reliability of any evaluation procedure depends on the quality of information obtained and the clinical skills of those who collect and interpret the information. A complete and comprehensive assessment process that utilizes information from various sources is a fundamental safeguard against drawing incorrect conclusions that may harm the child or jeopardize important relationships for the child.

The evaluator's attitude and behavior toward parents and child are primary influences on what and how much the family members are willing to share. Every effort must be made to ensure that each member of the family has an open opportunity to provide all information that may be useful in understanding the current problem. After the information is gathered, the evaluation team must have the necessary clinical expertise to interpret the information accurately.

OBTAINING QUALITY INFORMATION

At the onset of the evaluation, the evaluation team must take measures to ensure that the parents will have the confidence that the team will be honest to the process and that the process will provide definitive results about what may have happened to their child or what may have led to the mistaken belief that the child was abused. The parents must have confidence that the evaluators are neutral to the outcome and are acting in the best interest of the child.

The child must also perceive that the evaluators are neutral with respect to each parent and want to hear from the child what may have happened that has caused the trouble in his or her family. To avoid the possibility that the child sees the evaluators to be aligned with one parent or the other, both parents should be equally involved in the evaluation process. The child should be observed with each parent and should understand that the evaluators will have access to information from all members of the family. The child should also be made to understand that he or she will have opportunity to express to understanding people in a safe environment his or her feelings and experiences about parents and siblings.

The evaluators must establish trust with each parent during the evaluation process. This trust-building process begins with the first contact with each parent, even prior to the first face-to-face meeting. During that first meeting, the evaluators should give the parents an overview of what is involved in the evaluation process for them and their children. The parents are invited to ask questions about any part of the process. The parents also read and sign a consent form that outlines the procedures that will be used and the confidentially issues. They are informed that each session is being videotaped. (Please note that informed consent laws vary from state to state.)

The evaluator who sees the child with each parent must convey to the child that he or she will be kept safe during the evaluation process. This evaluator should help the child to recognize that he or she as well as the evaluator who will see the child in an individual play interview want to understand the child's experiences with each parent and with respect to the current allegations. At each transition point, the evaluator prepares the child for the next part of the evaluation process. The evaluator explains to the child that he or she will talk with the parents while the child plays in the same room and that the child will have a time to say what needs to be said when his or her parents are not present.

If the family is intact, the child and siblings are seen with both parents together. If the family is not intact, the child and siblings come for the first parent-child session with the custodial parent. The evaluator then prepares the child for the session with the noncustodial parent by telling him or her in the presence of the custodial parent that he or she will see father (or mother). The evaluator explains that the session will be similar to the one with the custodial parent. If the child expresses or shows any anxiety about being alone with the noncustodial parent, the evaluator agrees to stay with the child as long as the child needs him or her. When the child appears to be comfortable with the noncustodial parent, the evaluator seeks his or her permission before leaving the room.

During the interview, the evaluator must convey an openness to hearing what each parent has to say about the allegations or about any topic. Throughout the information-gathering process, the evaluation team must remain open to all possibilities: the child has been abused by the parent; the child has been abused by someone else; the child has not been abused; or the allegations are mistaken or malicious. All pertinent information must be considered before drawing conclusions about whether the child has been abused and, if so, by whom.

In the individual play interview, the evaluator must also convey to the child an openness to understand whatever the child has to communicate. The evaluator defines the purpose of the session and assures the child that the assessment is a safe environment in which to communicate. He or she communicates to the child an openness to listening to the child and that the child can speak through play as well as in words. The evaluator translates the child's actions into words and repeats back to the child the child's statements to assure the child that he or she has been heard. This also allows the child to correct any misperceptions. This process allows the child to continue to communicate experiences and perceptions.

Only when the child feels heard and understood can he or she leave the session with a sense of confidence that the problems in the family will be resolved. This sense of completion and confidence are communicated in words or behaviors. The child who leaves the sessions saying, "I all done," the child who tells the evaluator at the end of the play interview, "The power is with you," or the child who carries the dolls from the room where he or she has reenacted the trauma to a safe place are all communicating their confidence that the evaluator will help them resolve the current dilemma.

The evaluator must be careful not to influence what the child produces, whether verbally or behaviorally, during the interview. Yates (1991) explores the various ways an evaluator can influence the outcome of an interview with the child. The evaluator's influence may be subtle and yet powerful in influencing what the child discloses.

According to Yates (1991, p. 324) the child may be "overtly or covertly rejected for not providing the expected responses, or rewarded for providing the 'right' answer." The evaluator may "unwittingly prejudice the child by differentially" responding to certain responses, either responding with greater interest to sexual and violent material or uncritically accepting whatever the child produces. When this occurs, "the child quickly learns to offer the kinds of material that keep the interviewer enthusiastic and involved." As Yates explains, the evaluator has the difficult task of "chart(ing) a mid course" between uncritical acceptance of everything a child says and confronting the child. Uncritical acceptance may encourage fantasy; challenging or confronting the child may inhibit the child from producing relevant information.

The evaluator must be careful to avoid making premature judgments about the outcome of the evaluation process before all relevant information has been gathered and carefully considered. The evaluator should provide opportunity for each parent to provide information they believe pertinent to the present situation. The evaluator should be nonjudgmental and should not reinforce either parent for responses or behaviors during the interview. He or she should be open to hearing without prejudice what each parent has to say.

Steele (1991) suggests there is more of a taboo in talking about incest than about breaking the barrier itself. This reluctance to talk about child sexual abuse also holds true for evaluators and therapists who are more comfortable dealing with the crisis and current situation than in exploring how history is influencing current problems. Evaluators and therapists may join with or encourage their clients to reconstruct a more comfortable reality rather than to help them face the reality of their childhood trauma. If clients are not given permission to explore their childhood trauma within the safe, therapeutic environment, they must maintain the secret of their childhood pain in order to preserve their fragile sense of self and the respect of the therapist. They will continue to "unconsciously reenact the problem of their childhood in an effort to resolve past hurts" (D'Antonio, 1992, p. 149).

CLINICAL TRAINING TO INTERPRET
BEHAVIORAL OBSERVATIONS

Accurate interpretation of behavioral observations requires special clinical training or experience. This training is not typically a part of many clinical programs in clinical psychology, social work, or psychiatry. The implications of this lack of training are shown in recent research. Starr (1987) found that experienced clinicians could differentiate only at a chance level maltreating and nonmaltreating mothers based on a few minutes of video-taped interactions. Another study (Dietrich-McClean & Walden, 1988) showed that child protection workers were more capable of making these distinctions than were mental health experts.

These findings do not negate the value of observations of parent-child interactions in assessing experiences and attachment relationships. To the contrary, the greater reliability obtained by child protection workers, who routinely rely on observations of the child and family in the home and in neutral settings to make decisions about the safety of the child, suggests that experience in using observations enhances clinical skills. These studies demonstrate the need for experience and training to use observations effectively and the need for assessment protocols that include observation of relationships and behavior.

TRANSCRIPTION OF THE VIDEOTAPED
RECORD OF SESSIONS

The parent-child sessions and the play interview with the child must be videotaped. This will allow the evaluator to fully participate in each session and then, after the session is complete, to accurately and completely review and transcribe the verbal and behavioral content of each session. All transcription descriptions should be value-neutral. The transcription should be in a script form that is sufficiently detailed to allow the evaluator to recall and to cue what was said and done during the session. The transcription should include:

1. verbal statements;
2. physical behaviors;
3. eye contact or avoidance of eye contact;
4. spatial relationships;
5. proximities and touching;
6. affect, especially discordant affect between parent and child;
7. activities with people and objects;
8. content of drawings and the context in which they are drawn in terms of what is happening, either contemporaneously or in sequence;
9. willingness to engage each other and things fully; and
10. lack of action or response.

The transcription process and product are invaluable. The evaluator does not know before and during the sessions what information that is presented will be critical to understanding how the family came to the present situation; it is not until the information gathering is completed that an analysis can be initiated. To be of aid, the transcript must be complete, and it also must be without predetermination in terms of selective transcription of negative or positive behaviors or statements.

INTERPRETATION OF OBSERVATION AND INTERVIEW INFORMATION

Accurate interpretation of observation and interview material available in the Kempe Interactional Assessment requires training and experience. The evaluator's interpretation can then be articulately presented to others. Accurate interpretation begins with the complete, value-free transcript. Participants in the assessment have given verbal and behavioral evidence of experiences, perceptions, activities, and relationships; often this has been done without the participants having been consciously aware of the significance of the information.

In reviewing transcription notes, the evaluator looks for these recurrent patterns in observed behaviors, recurrent themes in parental responses to interview questions, and correlations among them. The validity of what each parent has reported can be determined by looking at consistency between observed behavior and with what the other parent has reported about the same events or experiences. Although each parent brings his or her own unique perspective to the assessment, there should be a basic consistency in what each has to report about the same incident or experience.

The evaluator should be alert to undercurrents or hints from the child and from the parents about experiences that may not be directly revealed but alluded to. The parents may use metaphors and stories to describe experiences and their cognitive distortions that remove any blame from them for their behavior to the child. Parents will give clues in the evaluation about their own childhood traumas that will need to be addressed in treatment. Children may use metaphors and stories as well. It is the cumulative information from different sources during the evaluation that make these stories and metaphors significant and meaningful in understanding what happened in the family and how the parents are interpreting the experience to themselves and to others.

It is significant when the parent does not deny the abuse but indicates that he or she does not remember this happening, suggests that the child may have misinterpreted "normal" behaviors as sexual behaviors, or claims that the child was the seducer. The parent who describes the child's sexual behavior toward him or herself, which he or she had to resist, is acknowledging the activity. The parent is, however, shifting the responsibility to the child for initiating the inappropriate behavior. As Steele (1991) points out, the adult is the one who breaks the incest barrier, not the child.

The evaluator should note signs of comfort or discomfort of the child with each parent and the situations in which the child appears to be more or less comfortable. Observable signs of the child's discomfort must be described to support the evaluator's belief that the child was uncomfortable or anxious. The source of that anxiety will then need to be determined based on all of the information available in the evaluation process.

The child's spatial relationship and involvement with the parent may change across the session. This change does not negate the behavior observed in one situation but must be considered in interpreting the nature of the child's experiences with the parent. Distancing and avoidance during reunion may be followed later by enmeshment in interactions that are regressed, sexualized, or inappropriate to a parent-child relationship.

The content of the behaviors of child and parents is as important as its observed impact on the other partner. A child's positive response to sexually stimulating or otherwise inappropriate behavior does not make the interactive sequence appropriate. The content is critical in understanding the child's experiences with the parent. The child brings his history of experiences with each parent into the evaluation session, and the child's behavior becomes a reliable index to the child's prior experiences with each parent.

The child's statements in response to directed questions, spontaneous statements, behaviors, symbolic play themes, drawings, metaphors, and stories are used to reconstruct the child's experience with each parent and to determine whether the child has been abused and by whom.

The child's responses to directed questions may be contradictory to information revealed in drawings, metaphors, stories, or in repeated themes in symbolic play. The child may give "expected" answers to directed questions in order to please the evaluator or a parent or even to avoid getting into trouble. The child's affect may provide clues to whether the child is disclosing past trauma or giving expected answers to questions without understanding the consequences of what he is saying.

Many children who have been abused by a parent cannot say directly in words what has happened to them. Younger children are more likely to disclose in words or behavior because they do not understand the consequences of such disclosures. As children get older, they are less likely to either directly or accidentally disclose the abuse. Not only do they have conflicted feelings about the abusive parent, but also they may feel guilty for their participation in the abuse. This is particularly the case if they received secondary gains from the abuse. The evaluator must be able to understand a child who expresses him or herself through play materials; this may be the child's only active medium of expression (Bresee, Stearns, Bess, & Packer, 1986).

CONCLUSION

The evaluation team members must be guided by general principles that inform good clinical practice. They must also have specific expertise from training and experience to obtain quality information and to interpret that information. The decision about whether a parent has sexually abused a child must be based on assessments of the parents, siblings, and the child who is the alleged victim.

The conclusions drawn about whether abuse occurred or did not occur as alleged will affect the child and all future relationships. If abuse occurred, the child must be protected from further sexual exploitation by the parent. If the child was abused by someone else, the child must be protected from the abuser while relationships are repaired within the family. If the child was not abused, then the child's relationship with the falsely accused parent needs to be preserved. The parent who mistakenly believed the other parent abused their child needs to be helped to accept that no abuse occurred. This may involve helping this parent to separate his or her own childhood trauma or issues with an ex-spouse from the child's experiences and relationship with the other parent.

The child's experiences must be validated in order for the healing process to begin for the child and family. This requires a skilled evaluator who can carefully obtain all information that is relevant to understanding how the child and family came to the present situation.

4

A Parent's Unresolved Childhood Trauma: Variations on a Theme

A parent's unresolved childhood trauma will affect current family relationships in ways that cause accusations or actual occurrence of parent-child sexual abuse. Case illustrations demonstrate how parents may actively recreate their own trauma with current family members and cause similar trauma for the children, or parents may be made passive by their own trauma and permit current family members to inflict and suffer trauma, or parents may project their own trauma onto current family members as if similar trauma in fact were occurring when it is not. The tragedy is that these dysfunctional patterns are carried from one generation to the next (Steele, 1970, 1983).

The parent's trauma cannot be resolved, the dysfunctional patterns cannot be changed, and appropriate therapy cannot be provided without an assessment that accurately determines whether and why parent-child sexual abuse occurred and, if it did not, why the accusation was made.

A parent's strategy for coping with unresolved childhood trauma, and the nature of the trauma itself, can be observed in the current attachment relationships and in the child's current behaviors and statements. These are the basis for an accurate assessment and appropriate therapy.

We recognize that the case descriptions presented in this and subsequent chapters are too abbreviated to provide a comprehensive view of all the factors involved. We discourage our readers from using these cases as models for making determinations of their own. They are illustrative of a significant issue, theory, or pattern that may be found in cases involving allegations of parent-child sexual abuse.

IDENTIFICATION WITH THE
NONPROTECTIVE PARENT

A mother who was a victim of sexual abuse by a parent or parent-figure may identify with her nonprotective parent. She may repeat the pattern of not protecting and blaming the child for the abuse. For example, a young girl (Alice) experienced chronic and severe sexual abuse from age 2 to 9 years of age by her mother's boyfriend. Although she told her mother of the abuse, it was only when she told teachers at school that steps were taken to protect her and her siblings. The case went to court, and the boyfriend was sentenced to a three-year prison term. A few months before he was to be released, the mother expressed her belief that he had not and would not molest any of her other children. She rationalized his sexual abuse of her oldest daughter as anger over her own sexual promiscuity:

> He didn't, he won't mess with his own....He told her it was out of anger. I was screwing around. She belongs to me not him. All these four belong to him. He wouldn't touch them.

The relationship with her sexually abusive boyfriend had priority over her relationship with her children:

He's the father of four of my kids. It's his responsibility to take care of them. He's going to be brought back into the house no matter what terms they're on. She knows he ain't gonna mess with her.

When asked how Alice knew that, her mother answered for her, "She's already told him." Alice, however, had no confidence that the abuse would not occur again:

I don't know that. I'm taking a chance. I'm not sure I'll be able to say anything next time it happens because all of the changes I went through before for telling it. Basically, I'm taking a chance.

This was the pattern this mother experienced with her mother. As a child her disclosure to her mother that mother's boyfriend was sexually abusing her led to her mother's rejection and abandonment of her:

The man's the head of the household. Girls are not supposed to express emotion except behind closed doors at certain times where a man can do whatever he wants because that's their status....[I was abused by] mother's boyfriend. [He] came in, started messing with me....It got to the point where I ran away. When I ran away, I was a CHINS [Child in Need of Supervision], locked up. When I turned 18 I was ready to go home. Just like Alice, either strong and surviving, or weak and faltering. My mother said I was a witch and she didn't want me home.

As a child, this mother had been excluded from the family and punished for being the victim. Not surprisingly, this mother reported that her mother had not believed her in the past and still did not believe her:

> She didn't believe me. She beat me under the bed with the broom and everything....My mom still asks, "Bob didn't do that." She still can't accept it.

Mother reported that at first Alice did not tell her about the abuse, and that when Alice did tell her, she did not believe her. When asked why she thought she could not see the abuse, the mother blamed her own history of abuse:

> I could have seen more if it hadn't happened to me. I put it in the back of my mind. If I had researched what happened to me I would have seen it sooner.

She coped with her childhood trauma by repressing painful memories. Her repression of her own childhood trauma prevented her from being able to see that her child was being traumatized in the same way she had been as a child.

PARENTS' TRAUMAS WEAVE TOGETHER

A mother, as a child, who was deprived of normal affection and attention from her own parents subsequent to their divorce, was pleased when her husband gave attention to their 3-year-old daughter, Jane. The mother had difficulty in seeing that the father's attention was sexual in nature and dismissed even an explicit statement of the daughter, "I had a dream last night that Daddy put his pooh in my mouth and it tasted yucky."

When Mother confronted Father about what their 3-year-old daughter had said, he denied the abuse and sought to intimidate the child by demanding to know what she told her mother.

Not surprisingly, the child said it was only a dream. Mother accepted Father's explanation that their daughter's words simply reflected her imagination.

Several changes were necessary before the mother was able to more objectively view her husband's relationship with their daughter. Although she was frustrated with a deterioration in her sexual relationship with her husband that coincided with the birth of their daughter and also resented what seemed to be her husband's efforts to isolate her from family and friends, she had to separate herself from her husband completely before she could see the disturbed nature of the relationships within their new family.

Mother's decision to take her daughter to visit her family provided a safe context for mother to re-evaluate her situation. She enjoyed more freedom for herself and for her then 4-year-old child. This also provided an opportunity for her to observe her child with other children and adults. She noticed that her child acted differently than the other children, that she flirted with men, initiated sexual games with same-age boys, pulled her panties down to make children laugh, and masturbated daily, often in public places, to an extent that did not seem normal to Mother.

With the encouragement and support of her family, Mother asked her daughter about experiences with Father. The child, also now in a safe environment, was able to say what Father had done in a very direct way. Her words as reported by Mother to others conveyed a child's perception of involvement in sexual activities with an adult. For example, she reported that she had to wash her father's "pooh" (word for penis) in the shower and some stuff came out. Other statements also indicated a child's perception of unusual events, such as her account of lying in a bed with her father's hands "loving her all over."

Mother's history provided insight into her attraction to her husband and to her subsequent failure to see his abuse of their child. As a neglected child, she craved but did not get attention from her mother or physically absent, alcoholic father. Part of the attraction to her husband was his attention to her. She was able to accommodate a shift in his attention from her to their child; having missed this attention herself as a child, she was pleased that her husband was invested in their child. In addition, she was completely financially and emotionally dependent on her husband. She could not risk loss of the only relationship she had. It was only after she had the support of her family and had gained some independence from her husband that she could accept the possibility that her husband had sexually abused their child.

Father's history also provided insight into the sexual abuse. Father, who had been emotionally deprived as a child, sought the closeness and affection he had not received as a child from his mother first with a teenage wife and then with his child. Although he was in his 30s, he had chosen a teenage partner whom he could control and mold into the person he wanted her to be. It was only after the birth of their daughter that he turned his interest and affection away from his wife to his daughter.

Although Father denied sexually abusing his daughter, his efforts to conceal his sexual involvement with his young daughter failed. Father suggested that his daughter imagined the abuse or herself produced the physical signs of penetration. But he also expressed a belief that his young daughter experienced the sexual abuse as attention and affection and that her desire for a relationship with him after a long separation would prevent her from disclosing the abuse.

The gentleness we have between us, a big plus....Distance makes the heart grow fonder. My main wish is that she will come through this stronger. Not so much the truth comes out, pray not so much her imagination but that she inflicted upon herself. I know it wasn't me. I'm hoping it didn't happen at all. I just want her to grow up strong and healthy. I'd like to add some selfish part to it and be a big part in her life.

Even if Father's explanations for the physical signs and the child's statements were plausible, his behavior with his child showed that he viewed her as a sexual object. For example, the reunion was spent with Father telling his daughter how beautiful she was and reminding her of gifts he had given and activities they had enjoyed together. He used various forms of trickery to entice his daughter to come close or to give him hugs and kisses.

Father's words and behavior with his young daughter were more appropriate to an estranged lover than to his own child. For example, when she gave him a hug, he responded, "I love it when you hold me." The message was that he needed her to fulfill his needs. He showed little understanding of her needs as a child and was unable to join her in activities that she selected. He ignored her wish to play and suggested that they talk much as one might expect adults to do.

It is not uncommon for children abused by their parents to have conflicted feelings about the abusive parent. They give various clues to their wish to have a relationship uncontaminated by the abuse. In the interactional assessment, this child expressed her wish to be a boy, a brother, or a son, as if this change in sex would normalize her relationship with her father.

PROJECTION OF CHILDHOOD TRAUMA ONTO CURRENT RELATIONSHIPS

Parents with unresolved childhood trauma may project their own experiences onto current relationships and believe current abuse is occurring when it is not. An illustrative example is a marriage including a woman who was sexually abused as a child by her father. As an adult, she was attracted to older men who, like her abusive father, would control her. She married a man 10 years her senior and became a child within her marriage rather than an equal partner.

The woman's incestuous relationship with her father interfered with her having a healthy sexual relationship during her marriage. A relationship that had been satisfying and healthy prior to marriage and sexual intimacy deteriorated afterwards. When she initiated sexual intimacy or enjoyed sex, she believed her husband viewed her as a "slut." When she was passive and allowed him to control the sexual intimacy, she resented what she perceived to be his using her to meet his needs, with little regard for her as a person. Her ambivalence about her sexual relationship with her father was reenacted in her relationship with her husband. The sexual intimacy with her husband either engendered guilt or resentment of his demands of her.

When her child Sam was born, two memories were evoked: what it had been like to be a child and how she herself had been parented (Steele, 1970). As the child grew, this mother repeated the pattern of care she had received as a child. She identified with her mother and rejected her son as she had been rejected by her mother as a child. Because she also identified her child with herself as a small child, she saw him as the child-victim who was seduced by Father before he had any understanding of right and wrong.

These distorted perceptions of the baby were enhanced because the baby was difficult to soothe. Mother could not comfort her crying baby and could not successfully breastfeed; Mother personalized the baby's difficult behavior to herself and came to believe that the baby accepted care from the father that he rejected from her.

A degenerating pattern developed as Mother became more frustrated with her failure to meet her baby's needs and directed her anger to the baby. Mother felt devalued and used by the baby just as she had first felt with her abusive father and then with her husband during sexual intimacy.

Mother resented her husband's success in comforting the baby when she could not and came to believe that the good relationship she observed between her husband and the baby was based on sexually inappropriate activities. She believed that the child, unaware of society's sanctions, experienced the sexual activities as Father's way of showing love to him, and rejected her because she would not show affection to him in the same sexualized way that father did.

Father who recognized legitimate reasons for the baby's difficulties did not recognize that Mother had personalized the baby's inability to breastfeed or to take normal formula. Mother's childhood sexual abuse was kept secret from her husband and from others who might have helped her resolve her own childhood trauma in order that she could view her baby's behavior more objectively.

By the time Mother first made allegations that Father had sexually abused their child, the relationship between Mother and her then 6-year-old son had deteriorated to the point that the son was predictably angry and rejecting of his mother. At age 9, he rejected his male identity, and at the same time he stated his intention to marry a boy when he grew up. To understand his confusion, one must look at what it had meant to him to be a boy. In some sense, he felt his mother had rejected him because he was a boy. He believed that if he had been a girl, his mother might have loved him and cared for him as she cared for his younger sisters or as his father was able to care for him as a boy. Because the most satisfying relationship had been with Father, he hoped to find someone like Father who would give him the same sense of being cared for and loved as his father had. This relationship was not sexual, but simply one in which Father's emotional availability and acceptance had led to a mutually satisfying father-son relationship.

Each parent's childhood gave clues to their very different attitudes and behavior toward their son. To help a family such as this heal, a therapist needs to have access to historical information as well as the information about the presenting problem. A different course of therapy is needed if Mother is projecting her own history of rejection by her mother and inappropriate attention from Father onto current relationships with her child and husband. The mother needs someone to give her permission to confront her childhood trauma. Without this permission, she will continue to "consciously avoid revealing [her] experiences or unconsciously repress and deny them out of shame and fear of disapproval" (Steele, 1991, p. 16).

CONCLUSION

Unresolved issues from childhood trauma may be played out in different ways. The birth of a child or the child's sex, age, or behavior may evoke memories of the parent's own childhood trauma. Parents cope differently with the flood of memories brought back by their child.

Parents victimized as children who value (or need) a relationship with an abusive spouse may identify with their nonprotective parent and repeat that parent's pattern of not believing or blaming the child.

Parents deprived of their own parent's attention and affection may be seduced by other persons who give them the affection and attention of which they have been deprived. These parents may not be able to see the inappropriate nature of the relationship of their spouses with their children until they are able to gain support of others outside the family and to be more objective in interpreting the meaning of their child's behaviors and statements that are consistent with involvement in adult sexual activities.

Parents who have repressed or have not resolved their childhood trauma may project their experiences onto current relationships and mistakenly believe their spouse is abusing their child.

The three cases in this chapter illustrate the different ways in which the parents attempt to cope with childhood trauma and how these different coping strategies influence their choices of partners and their attitudes and behaviors toward their children. Therapy for each family member must take into account the unique trajectory through which the family came to the present situation. This means understanding the current situation in relation to the history of each parent in their families of origin as well as their history as a couple and as parents.

5

Mothers and Grandmothers: Thinking the Unthinkable

Accurate interpretation of the data collected during the assessment requires careful consideration of each of the family relationships. The two cases in this chapter illustrate situations in which an evaluator is presented with deliberate efforts to confuse the child and others about the existence of abuse and the identity of the perpetrator.

Incomplete or nonobjective assessments cannot reliably determine what in fact has occurred. An assessment conducted in the conceptual framework of family attachment relationships—including observation of the child with each person and significant adult in the child's life—is essential to accurate and reliable assessment. These case illustrations demonstrate that such an assessment may yield unanticipated results.

A NAME THAT SOUNDS LIKE "DADDY"

Mother reported to her pediatrician that 3-year-old Melanie made an outcry during her "cleaning" of the child, after which mother noticed some redness in the child's vaginal area. Medical examination indicated a small amount of erythema and bruising of the hymenal ring but showed no indication of penetration. The pediatrician reported suspected sexual abuse of the child to Child Protection Services, and based on Mother's report of what Melanie purportedly had said to her, he indicated Melanie's father as the probable perpetrator. A Dependency and Neglect Petition was filed. Preliminary orders gave temporary physical custody to Mother, and precluded father from any form of contact with Melanie. Mother's family continued to have access to the child but Father's family did not.

The initial investigation by Child Protection Services was considered to be inconclusive with respect to whether and by whom Melanie had been sexually abused; Melanie was placed in investigative play therapy to facilitate further disclosure. During the next 6 months of investigative therapy, Melanie's therapist did not obtain psychiatric, psychological, or other evaluations of the parents nor did she consult with other professionals. The investigator-therapist did not obtain complete histories of the parents or other adults significant in Melanie's life. Significant aspects of the histories that were obtained were ignored; these included the troubled and platonic nature of the mother and father's relationship, the mother's ongoing lesbian relationship with a lover, the mother's rage at discovering that the father had a female lover, and the existence of a maternal relative named Danny.

During the investigation, the therapist followed her usual practice of receiving information from the accusing mother, but refusing to talk with or observe the accused father. She justified not observing the father with the child, stating: "I am not trained to assess adults and I am not trained to assess adult-child interactions. I am simply trained to assess the child." The investigator-therapist explained that seeing Melanie with her father would not be helpful to her in determining if the father abused her:

> Many perpetrators are very skillful in scaring their children, the children they have abused, with threats or intimidation, so children are usually afraid of that....I am not sure [that Father's presence or participation in sessions with Melanie] would provide real clear information....I guess I'm thinking that Melanie, if she saw her dad, might be real excited to see him and she might run over and jump up on his lap and give him a big hug, and you know, be real appropriate together in the evaluation, or whatever, and I'm not sure what that would mean.

Nonetheless, although not permitting the father to participate, the therapist conducted many sessions in which the mother was present and participating. The therapist downplayed evidence that the mother might have prompted or coerced the child into making statements accusing the father; this evidence included a tape recording of the mother and a friend telling the child: "You need to tell or you will be taken away from your mommy, you'll go to live with your daddy, you'll never see us again..." The therapist dismissed the coercive possibilities of such statements, saying:

> All they did was frighten [Melanie]. I don't think they put words in her mouth, they didn't tell her what to say or they weren't leading in the aspect of telling her what to say.

The investigator-therapist's assessment was further complicated because Mother affirmatively withheld information that the situation was not as clear as she had originally presented it; this information might have helped others determine what had happened to Melanie.

After her first marriage ended in divorce, mother became sexually involved with another woman also going through a divorce. She met Melanie's father during a separation from her lesbian lover. Although she enjoyed fishing and hunting with him, she reported that she was never attracted to him sexually. Father learned about her lesbian relationship at the same time he learned that she was pregnant with his child. The couple did not marry; however, Mother had on occasion taken Melanie and lived in Father's house with him when she was in conflict with her lesbian lover.

Also, during a deposition Mother acknowledged that after Melanie's outcry, Melanie had used the words "good daddy" to refer to her father. When asked what else Melanie had said about her "good daddy," Mother stated:

> She has said that good daddy does things for her, good daddy is sad and good daddy is sorry that this has happened.

When asked what Melanie had said about "bad daddy," Mother replied, "Bad daddy has hurt her." When she was asked to describe what Melanie had said about someone whose name sounds like daddy, Mother reported that Melanie had told her that the person whose name sounds like daddy, "was there taking pictures," and then added, "(He) hurt her with Dad." When asked if she knew anyone with this name, Mother named a young boy she knew and then almost as an afterthought named her relative whose given name was Danny.

Mother's diary also contained information about changes in Melanie that began during and continued after a visit to her maternal grandparents', during which time she had contact with Danny. This visit occurred immediately after Mother discovered Father's relationship with another woman and a few days before Mother's outcry on behalf of Melanie.

In her diary Mother reported that after her return from her grandparents' home, Melanie was afraid to go to sleep and worried that someone was watching them. In the weeks after Mother reported the abuse, Melanie continued to do and say things that indicated exposure to and participation in adult sexual activities. Once when in the bathroom with Mother, she asked Mother to check to see if there were "sticky juice" on her arm and on the wall. She talked about being tied down, being naked on television with someone whose name sounded like "Daddy," someone putting his mouth on her pee pee, and someone hurting her in the shower. Melanie repeatedly asked about her "good daddy," whom she wanted to come to protect them from being hurt.

The therapist not only relied exclusively on information filtered through Mother—who believed or wanted others to believe that Father was the abuser—she also disregarded Melanie's direct communications that did not fit with a conclusion that Melanie's father had sexually abused her.

> Okay, I asked her if she could make a picture...of her family, and she did, but her drawings were so simple due to her age that I didn't keep them. It was basically just circles, nothing significant came out of the drawings....I asked her if there was anyone else in her family and she said, "Daddy."

The therapist threw away the drawings.

Melanie's efforts to tell the therapist that her "good daddy" and "bad daddy" were different people failed. For example, Melanie said her daddy fed her, put her to bed, and also bathed her. She then said that a person, with a name heard as "Daddy," did not feed her or put her to sleep but did bathe her. On another occasion, the therapist showed Melanie family pictures. One picture included Danny. Melanie named the other relatives without hesitation but paused before naming him. The pause was significant enough for the therapist to make a note of it. She did not interpret Melanie's hesitation as a sign of anxiety but concluded that Melanie probably did not know this person as well as the others.

With the pictures of the family members spread out in front of them, the therapist asked Melanie who hurt her. Melanie pointed to the picture of her daddy, and said,

Not my good daddy, not my good daddy, just bad "daddy."
One daddy, good daddy, he not daddy, just bad daddy.

The therapist interpreted Melanie's words to mean that she had split her daddy into a good and a bad daddy.

After almost 6 months of seeing Melanie, the therapist concluded that Melanie had been sexually abused, and that her father was the perpetrator of the abuse. The therapist explained to Melanie that she understood that Melanie wanted to believe her good daddy did not hurt her. She stated that she, however, believed that Melanie's daddy had hurt her. During her deposition, the therapist explained her decision to tell Melanie good and bad daddy were the same person:

Well, I guess at that point I sort of switched from being an investigator to being an therapist and I thought therapeutically she needed to deal with that issue then and there, and I think we did and I think she benefited from it, and so that's what we did.

Based on a stipulation between the parents, the Court entered an order that

the child's environment is injurious to her welfare....[She] is a severely disturbed child....[Her environment] may include sexual abuse, emotional, and psychological abuse.

Father continued to deny that he abused Melanie but agreed to participate in any evaluations that might be useful in determining what had happened to Melanie. The Court ordered psychological tests of the parents, a plethysmographic assessment of Father, and interactional assessments of Melanie with each parent.

The father's psychological evaluation indicated "generally good adult functioning" with "no indications of characterological impulsivity, antisocial behavior, narcissism or other traits or behavior patterns that would predispose toward 'sick' behavior." The results of the plesthysmographic assessment showed that Father's "arousal pattern [did] not appear supportive of current pedophilic interest related to female children" and that his "auditory profile consistently demonstrated high arousal to themes involving consensual sexual behavior with female adults and relatively low levels of arousal associated with themes involving sexual behavior with female children."

Mother's psychological report indicated considerable psychological problems for her related to her childhood history:

[Mother was] raised in an alcoholic household and began having interpersonal problems early in her life....There are clearly significant problems in her adjustment, with strong narcissistic traits coupled with histrionic emotionalism and other maladaptive behaviors. She has a paranoid orientation toward the world, seeing it as a threatening place in which she gets a raw deal. She is likely to blame others for her problems and lacks insight into herself.

The Kempe Interactional Assessment unequivocally demonstrated that Father and Melanie had a healthy attachment relationship that could be eliminated from suspicion of sexual abuse, but that Mother's own unresolved issues were interfering with her ability to develop a nurturing and protective relationship with Melanie. Mother would remain suspect either as the abuser or complicit in hiding the identity of the abuser.

Excerpts from Melanie's play interview, from the interactive session with Melanie and her mother, and from the interactive session with Melanie and her father illustrate how the various pieces of information were woven together to reconstruct Melanie's history with each parent and how each parent's history of being parented had influenced his or her relationship with Melanie.

Melanie communicated to the evaluator during the play interview that her mother's perception of what had happened to her was neither accurate nor consistent with her own experiences.

> *Evaluator.* Whom do you live with?
>
> *Melanie.* (*moving away from evaluator*) My mom. My dad hurt me.
>
> *Evaluator.* Your dad hurt you? How did your dad hurt you? What did he do?
>
> *Melanie.* I don't know.
>
> *Evaluator.* You don't know?
>
> *Melanie.* Huh huh. (*affirmative*)
>
> *Evaluator.* Did somebody say your dad hurt you?
>
> *Melanie.* I don't know....
>
> *Evaluator.* You said your daddy hurt you. I'm wondering how your daddy hurt you.
>
> *Melanie.* I don't remember how my daddy hurt me.
>
> *Evaluator.* You can't remember how your daddy hurt you?
>
> *Melanie.* No.

Then, communicating to the evaluator her actual experience of daddy's nurturing of her, Melanie put a baby doll, with which she was playing, in a chair by a table and announced, "They're gonna eat." She instructed the evaluator to join them at the table with a baby doll of her own and then stated, "Babies gonna have to sit in everybody's lap so they don't fall over." She then pretended that the baby sneezed and gently wiped its nose with a Kleenex. Melanie's words and actions conveyed her experiences of being protected from being hurt and of being nurtured by someone who held her in his lap and cared for her when she was sick.

Melanie continued her playing by pretending she was Mommy and the evaluator was the baby; the evaluator took advantage of this to explore what "Mommy" thought had happened to the baby.

Melanie, in the role of Mommy, pretended she was talking to the baby who was at Grandma's house. Melanie picked up a telephone and directed the evaluator to the other one. She greeted the evaluator with "Hi Baby," and then asked how the baby was doing. The evaluator asked Melanie what the baby should say, and Melanie told her to say "Fine." The evaluator then asked Melanie in her role as Mommy, "Mommy, do you think Daddy hurt me?" Melanie answered, "Yes." When the evaluator asked, "How did he hurt me, Mommy?" Melanie clearly and without hesitation stated, "On your pee pee." When the evaluator repeated, "On my pee pee," and then asked, "What did he do to my pee pee?" Melanie terminated the conversation, hung up the phone, and announced, "I came back."

Melanie's confusion, and her direct recognition of her father's confusion, about her mother's accusation was expressed toward the end of the session. The telephone conversation began with Melanie's pretending that Daddy was talking to Grandpa and ended with Melanie's screaming, "I don't know," as she held her little girl doll to the telephone and instructed the evaluator to have the daddy doll say it also.

For several minutes at the top of her voice and with great enthusiasm, Melanie screamed "I don't know." Melanie then asked the evaluator to scream it with her, and they screamed in unison, "I don't know." Everyone had placed the entire weight on Melanie, and it was beyond her capabilities to clear up the confusion.

Melanie's behavior during reunion with Mother showed that she had not had the kinds of experiences with Mother that enabled her to rely on Mother to meet her needs. Without greeting or looking at her mother, she went directly to the puzzles at the table across the room from where Mother was seated on the couch.

As she began to remove the puzzle pieces, her mother approached her, and after standing behind her for a moment dropped to her knees to help her with the puzzles. The puzzles were symbolic of the task facing Melanie and her mother. Melanie needed her mother's help in solving the current confusion, but her mother's actions only served to further confuse matters. When Melanie asked for help in placing puzzle pieces, her mother either offered no help, with "Gee I don't know," or gave incorrect advice that would lead to incorrect placement of the puzzle pieces.

Mother's memories of childhood showed a history of unsatisfying relationships with the exception of her relationship with Father as a child. She gave few details of childhood, but did recall that her father "used to spoil me rotten and took me places." She gave no description of her mother and negative descriptions of relationships with her siblings. She did not fit in with other girls in high school and felt rejected by boys who showed no interest in her.

As a teenager, she also became aware of her father's promiscuity. She experienced his affairs with other women not only as a betrayal of her mother but also of her. When she was asked if anything like what had happened to Melanie had happened to her as a child, Mother gave the incongruous response: "No, thank God for that, I think that would be the only thing I'd change (*laughs*)."

Mother's description, in the clinical interview, of Melanie's birth, revealed memories of her own childhood trauma, of being forced to do something she did not wish to do and being helpless to resist:

> The doctor made me watch her come out, because I was bearing down, they kept telling me to watch. I said, "No, no, no, just get her out." So he said, "I'll just hold her up until you look." I looked, watched her come out.

Her description of what happened after Melanie was placed on her stomach after delivery revealed her fear that Melanie would be hurt and that she would not be able to protect her even if present because of her own emotional pain:

> He laid her on my tummy. She went right away to my breast, grabbed the scissors, and started pulling those in her mouth. I went, "Oh oh oh, Lisa, do something for me." She got the scissors out. I was hemorrhaging pretty bad.

This was a self-fulfilling prophecy. Angered by Father's relationship with another woman and perceiving the relationship to be a betrayal of her and Melanie, Mother took Melanie away from him and left her in a place where she herself had been hurt as a child. Paradoxically, when asked what she would like to change if she could change anything in her life, Mother wished she had had "the insight to see that the abuse would have happened" and could have prevented it:

> Only one thing, for the abuse never to have occurred. God had given me insight to see it would have happened and I would have been able to prevent it, not let it happen.

During the course of the interview Mother's unusual references to "cleaning" and the pleasure she seemed to associate with this activity raised questions about the nature of Mother's own relationship with Melanie. Mother gave a somewhat unusual account of the circumstances in which Melanie disclosed her father's abuse of her:

> Well, I was getting ready for work and I was gonna go clean her up, noticed she was pretty red in doing so, like I say I was getting ready for work. She had gone potty, she didn't have any underclothes on, panties. I looked down and noticed she was pretty red and inflamed. "Guess we better clean you up a little before we get dressed." That's when she told me not to go inside her, which led me to think like I asked her if anybody had gone inside her.

Mother discounted another name given by Melanie that sounded like "Daddy," and in her account, indicated that Melanie finally said that "Daddy" went inside her.

"Cleaning" had been an activity Mother performed since Melanie was a small baby, and Mother's description of this routine suggested its special significance to her as a way of achieving closeness and intimacy with Melanie:

> We got into a pretty good routine: mostly in the wee hours of the morning we'd get up, I'd clean her and change her, and then we'd go down and lay on the couch (*sighs*), find the most comfortable position for breastfeeding.

After she cleaned and changed Melanie, she was then able to provide some semblance of nurturing in breastfeeding Melanie.

Mother's response to a question about whether she would like to raise Melanie in the same way she herself had been raised showed her focus on the lack of normal intimacy and affection in her family.

> Yes, I do, only a couple of little things I would change and I think we're doing real well with that, that is our family

was never really a touchy family or a hugging family, "I love you" family, we were all pretty much out of school before that started up, make sure I tell her I love her several times throughout the day and give her several hugs and lots of contact in that way.

Although she wanted to give Melanie the sense of being loved that she had never experienced as a child in normal displays of affection, she was showing intimacy and closeness in the only way she had experienced it as a child, that is, in the context of sexual intimacy with a parent.

At the end of Melanie's session with Mother, the evaluator explained to Melanie that she would be seeing her father the next day. Melanie showed no distress and even named various toys present in the room that she wanted to be there for the day her daddy came.

The next morning, however, she seemed apprehensive as she stood outside the assessment room, clutching her mother's and grandmother's hands. Mother reported that Melanie was fearful about seeing her father and asked if she could remain nearby in case Melanie should need her. However, Melanie separated easily from her Mother and Grandmother and, once out of sight of Mother and Grandmother, was eager to join her Father, even declining an offer of juice prior to seeing him.

Father had seated himself on the floor of the assessment room facing the door as he waited quietly for Melanie to join him. When Melanie entered the room, Father greeted her with, "Hi Pumpkin." Melanie said, "Hi," as she walked to him and put her arms around his neck to hug him. Father asked, "How have you been?" and then said, "Gee I've missed you." Melanie responded, "Fine," before giving her daddy a kiss to his lips.

Melanie stood beside her daddy as he enclosed her loosely in a supportive way with his arm. He commented on how big she was getting and asked what she had been doing. She responded, "Not a heck of a lot." Father laughed as he repeated her words, "Not a heck of a lot."

Father then explained they were going to spend some time together. Over the next several minutes Father listened as Melanie shared with him experiences with kittens, rabbits, fishing, and the horses. Father told her there were toys they could play with in the room and asked if she wanted to get a toy to play with. Melanie replied, "Not yet," as she continued to stand near him with her hand resting on his shoulder. She had missed him and simply wanted to have this time to be close and to talk with him.

A few minutes later, when Melanie did decide to play with toys, she brought them to where Father was sitting. She first wanted him to read the book he had brought and, as he began to read, settled herself comfortably into his lap. After several stories, she went to get a puzzle and brought it back to where he was sitting. She stayed close to him throughout the session, often sitting on his lap, and seeking his help or participation in various play activities.

Father's ability to listen to her, to understand and reflect what she said, to provide effective help when she requested and needed it, and to join her in reenactment of activities shared in the past were in striking contrast to what was observed with her mother the previous day. Melanie's animated, spontaneous, and interactive behavior with Father was in striking contrast to her previous sober demeanor and tendency for isolated, independent play in the session with Mother.

As she had done the previous day, the evaluator obtained Melanie's permission to talk with the parent who was present while Melanie played. Father was protective of Melanie as he answered questions. He provided information the evaluator would need to understand his perspective while shielding Melanie from information not appropriate for her to hear. For example, when asked to say what he thought was going on with regard to the allegations, he responded in a soft voice as he sat behind Melanie on the floor,

> I feel a person is very insecure; when someone else came into my life they were afraid of losing (*points to Melanie and when Melanie turns around to look at him, he playfully touches her cheek and smiles*). This is as much as I can figure out.

Mother's responses to interview questions the previous day confirmed the accuracy of what Father believed had triggered the allegation. In responding to a question about whether Father was involved in other relationships during the time she and Melanie had lived with him, Mother reported getting angry when she learned Melanie might have met Father's girlfriend. She decided to take Melanie to her own parent's home while she considered what conditions she wanted to put on Melanie's father's seeing her.

Mother reported that when she told Melanie about her decision to take her to visit her grandparents, Melanie got very upset and said, "You're going to take me away from my daddy." She reassured Melanie, "No, I'm not gonna take you away from your daddy. We're just gonna go down and see Grandpa and Grandma."

When asked if these allegations had come up previously, Father described Mother as being preoccupied with the possibility he would abuse Melanie from the time of her birth:

> Abuse is something she's preoccupied with, brought up several times. Why does she have this preoccupation? Something I've never been able to figure out.

Mother herself reported that she had told Father the only reason she would ever take Melanie away from him would be if he abused her physically or sexually. Not surprisingly, she was unable to say why she worried that he might abuse Melanie.

As Father responded to a question about what he enjoyed with Melanie as a baby, Melanie reenacted her experiences of being nurtured by Father. She brought a doll to her father and placed it in Father's lap saying, "Baby wants you." Father lifted Melanie into his lap, commenting that he would hold her while she held the doll. Melanie fed the doll the bottle and then pretended the baby had a cold: "She coughed; she's got a runny nose." She wiped the doll's nose and noted, "The baby blowed it."

During this play sequence, Father's description of what he enjoyed with Melanie showed his sensitivity to her as a person and his commitment to being a good father:

> When she was real small, I'd initially spend time playing around the house with whatever toys or whatever she was interested in. As she got older, depending on what she was interested in, with colds, we did go through a lot of times with colds. When she was well I tried to get her outside as much as possible because I'd get tired of being cooped up in the house, and I think she did too, so I did try to get outside. I always enjoyed outdoors anyway. When permitted, to do as much outside as possible, summer go fishing, have a picnic or something. Inside, evenings when I had her to myself, it was hectic. I'd pick her up from work, go home, have dinner, give her a bath and then it was bedtime. After all that, I'd sit down and (*affective demonstration*) I can relax now. The weekend I tried to keep free. The week was hectic. I'd try to get the house cleaned up, do as much as I could in the week, plus take care of her so weekends were as free as possible and I'd be able to spend time with her, go and do, take her to the races and stuff like that.

Later when Father responded to a question about what he would change if he could change anything in his life, Melanie's words and actions showed her confidence that Daddy could clear up the confusion and also her expectation that he could and would take care of her.

As Father described his wish to change the current situation and to get back to normalcy, Melanie (who was sitting in the high chair) announced, "I spilled." Father helped her clean up the spill and continued his response by saying he wanted Melanie to have visitation with her mother, but worried about Mother having responsibility for the care of a child, given Mother's insecurity and instability.

In a demonstration to others that her daddy could meet her needs, Melanie called loudly, "I want milk now." As observed throughout the session, Father was able appropriately to divide his attention among himself, the evaluator, and Melanie and promptly responded to her by pouring her a glass of milk.

At the end of the session, Father left the room and Melanie waited with the evaluator while her mother returned. Melanie's efforts to share her good experiences with her "good daddy" were not successful; Mother did not or could not understand what Melanie was trying to communicate. Melanie's first words to Mother were a cheerful, "I played with my dad, he smiled at me, and he was good." Mother tersely replied, "Good, I'm glad to hear that it was a good visit."

As if sensing that Father might no longer be the suspect for the abuse, Mother asked, in a casual tone that did not disguise the painful nature of the question, if she was correct in remembering that the evaluator asked Mother the previous day if Melanie had mentioned anyone other than her daddy as the abuser. When the evaluator confirmed that she had indeed asked that question and asked it again, Mother replied:

Yes, about a month or so afterward she mentioned a person named Danny taking pictures of her and Daddy. I don't know who that would be.

The evaluator questioned what Mother meant by pictures and Mother elaborated: "Videotape, with her and Daddy naked on television." Although previously Mother had mentioned a relative with the name Danny, she now claimed she did not know anyone with that name and would not pursue this line of inquiry further.

As Melanie was about to leave the room with Mother, she picked up the book her father had brought for her and said, "Daddy brought this for me." Mother heard instead "Grandpa," and Melanie tried to correct her, saying, "No, my daddy, he's a special guy." Mother, expressing her own bittersweet and conflicted feelings about her father and about Melanie's father, asked, "Is he a special guy?" Melanie's spontaneous expression of affection for her "good daddy" in "I love him," seemed to strike a chord with Mother. Mother's affection for her own abusive father, and her resignation to the fact that Melanie did not consider her father to be an abuser, was expressed in Mother's response: "I know you do, sweetie."

As Melanie preceded her mother in leaving the room at the end of this session, she emphatically announced to someone in the hall, "I all done." She had told her story and believed someone had heard.

Melanie's therapist reported that Melanie was "real up" and "happy" when she saw her for the first time after Melanie's visit with her father during the interactional assessment. She attributed this to Melanie's wish to have a relationship with Father. She reported that Melanie assured her he was her "good daddy" and did not hurt her when she saw him.

Although the allegation that Father had sexually abused

Melanie was not substantiated in court, custody remained with Mother after the interactional assessment despite testimony from several experts that she was the more disturbed and less stable parent. Father was not awarded custody until almost a year later when Mother was arrested and placed on probation for sexual molestation of an adolescent girl.

The tragedy of this case and others like it is the readiness of both mental health professionals and the legal system to believe that fathers or men are the perpetrators and their resistance to believe that women or mothers would sexually abuse a child or shield an abuser.

A GRANDMOTHER'S SEXUAL INVOLVEMENT WITH HER GRANDDAUGHTER

The outcry came from a maternal grandmother based on a conversation with her granddaughter, 4-year-old Becky. The granddaughter's question to her grandmother about whether she had played "heinie" games when she was little led the grandmother to wonder whether her granddaughter was being sexually abused by her father. When Grandmother asked what she meant, Becky explained, "To play with the front side of your heinie," and then asked, "Did you know that Mommy played heinie when she was a little girl?"

Although this conversation was consistent with Becky's sex play with same-age cousins the previous summer, and consistent with her mother's explaining that she also had done this as a child, Grandmother immediately concluded that Becky's father had abused Becky and reported her concerns to Child Protective Services.

At the time of the initial report by Grandmother, there were no physical signs of sexual abuse. When questioned by the social worker, Becky made no verbal disclosure. Even so, Grandmother was successful in getting Becky's mother and others to believe that her father had abused Becky. Father was required to move out of the family home, and the couple subsequently divorced. In domestic relations court, Mother was awarded custody, and Father was allowed supervised visits with his daughter.

Almost two years later when normal contact was resumed with Father, Becky returned from an overnight visit with Grandmother with blood in her panties. She complained of hurting when she urinated. Physical examination revealed a "penetrating vaginal injury." This contrasted with the absence of physical findings when Becky was examined two years previously at age 4. Once again, Father was investigated for child sexual abuse even though Becky denied her father had hurt her and indeed had no memory of how she had been hurt.

During the course of the interactional session with Becky and her mother, it became clear that Grandmother played a key role both in creating misperceptions about what had happened to Becky and as an actor in the actual abuse of Becky. A key was that the physical symptoms occurred after a visit between Becky and Grandmother. During the interview, Mother described her surprise in a recent change in her daughter's feelings about Grandmother. She reported that Becky did not want to stay after dark at her grandmother's house and did not want to sleep there. When asked why she did not want to spend the night with Grandmother, Becky could only say that she wanted to be with her mommy.

Becky's behavior and statements during the session with Mother indicated that although she was uncomfortable with spending the night with Grandmother, she had no conscious awareness of the cause of this discomfort. At one point, Becky asked her mother how the doctor knew someone did something. Mother explained to her that her "vagina looked as if someone put something in there." Becky tearfully and firmly replied, "No one did." A while later she showed unusual interest in her mother's account of a time when medication made her memory "funny." Mother recalled that when she gave birth to Becky, the doctor gave her "medication, very strong medication" that "made me kind of woozy and it made my memory funny."

Becky interrupted her play to ask, "What was your memory like?" Mother explained, "It was hard for me to remember things that were going on at the time." Becky responded, "That's why you wanted to get out of there." Becky's words seemed to express her own anxiety associated with Grandmother and her not remembering what happened to her that caused this anxiety.

Everyone believed her father had hurt her, although this did not appear to be consistent with Becky's experiences with him. When Mother began to tell what she believed happened, Becky tearfully screamed at Mother,

> You don't ever let me say one word,...you're telling every-
> one in the whole world, all your friends. I don't want to
> hear this story again.

When it was clear that mother could not comfort her daughter nor let go of the story, the evaluator suggested that they leave this topic and talk about some early history with her daughter. Becky was then able to calm down and to help recall good memories of being the little baby girl her mother loved and valued.

During the session with Grandmother, Becky expressed discomfort in being alone with Grandmother or in leaving Grandmother alone to talk with the evaluator. She refused to enter or stay in the room where her grandmother was without the evaluator or her mother being present. Later she did not want to leave her grandmother alone with the evaluator.

After Becky left with her mother, Grandmother explained her granddaughter's reluctance to leave her alone with the evaluator: "She's very fearful of something being said she's not made aware of." When asked to say why her granddaughter might be

worried about what was said to others when she was not listening, Grandmother replied,

> She's been put in a situation not common for
> children...she's been going to a psychologist for a year...and
> her experience of the rape and child abuse prior to that
> was most unusual.

Recall that Grandmother's report of a conversation with her
granddaughter originally led to allegations of sexual abuse that
resulted in her loss of Father and her parents' divorce.

When asked how she accounted for the physical findings,
Grandmother responded, "In my mind no question her father
did it...he penetrated her with his penis." Grandmother was
unable to consider that someone else might have abused her
granddaughter. Grandmother was asked if she had ever observed
her granddaughter's masturbation that had been described by
Mother. Initially, she denied she had observed this, stating that
Becky did not do it at her house. She then recalled a time when
Becky was sleeping in her bed with her:

> Yes, I have, in her sleep, about age 5, she and I were in bed
> together, she woke up, she was not conscious, in a sleep
> state, I would say she went to orgasm, lay back down and
> went to sleep.

When asked if she believed Becky had any memory of what
happened to her, Grandmother stated she believed she did but
could not say because of her love for her father:

> Yes and some day, I don't know when, she'll name him. It
> must be terribly difficult for a little child who has these
> ambivalent feelings, I love my Dad, he should be a fine man,
> and yet this has happened to me, so despicable we don't

speak of it. I got the feeling that (*sighs*) it was so horrible she couldn't entertain it on a conscious level. I was glad when you gave permission so to speak.

Grandmother denied she had been sexually abused as a child, although she showed a fascination with celebrities who had recently disclosed sexual abuse by their fathers. She reported that she grew up in a "well-respected" family that was religious and had the "outward appearance of having good moral values." She stated that living in a small town "put a harness on kids, because you were aware of what other people think and of your reputation" whereas in a city people are "pretty much anonymous."

Mother accepted Grandmother's belief that her ex-husband sexually abused their child in much the same way she accepted Grandmother's perception of Grandfather. Although she was 10 years old when her father divorced her mother, this mother had no memories of him separate from what her mother had told her.

Mother's recognition of Grandmother's pathologic influence on her was reflected in her words to her daughter about mothers and daughters: "That's what mothers are here for, to make their daughters crazy." Even though this was said in a joking way, its truth could not be ignored. Grandmother was destroying the respective relationships of both mother and daughter with ex-husband and father just as she had destroyed her relationship and that of her daughter with grandfather.

Becky's experiences with Mother may have been very similar to Mother's experiences as a little girl with Grandmother. Becky said she would like to make her mother into a nice mother and then playfully described her as sometimes like a *bunny*, sometimes like a *rattle snake* and at other times like a *turtle*. This described her mother's mood swings from playfulness to sudden anger to depression and unavailability.

The sexual abuse allegations against Father were unsubstantiated by the court. The issue of the maternal grandmother's sexual involvement with her granddaughter was not directly addressed in the court findings. Grandmother was not a party to the case, and the court's findings were directed toward protecting the child by ordering supervised contact between Becky and her maternal grandmother.

Tragically, the therapists for Mother and Grandmother continued to believe and to work with their clients on the assumption that Father had abused his daughter and that Grandmother had been maligned by unfounded suspicion.

CONCLUSION

The two cases presented in this chapter illustrate how a mother and grandmother who grew up in incestuous families were preoccupied with the belief that their own experiences of betrayal by their fathers would be repeated in new father-child relationships. Fathers who grew up in families in which no abuse occurred did not know how to interpret this preoccupation. They had no framework in their own experiences for understanding what this meant and naively believed that the problem would resolve with time.

The real abuse of the child by someone other than the accused, or the child's normal sexual curiosity, provided the opportunity for the mother and grandmother to make an outcry on behalf of the child. Professionals who were biased to believe that men, and not women, do this, accepted that the father was the abuser—without adequately investigating family history, without questioning events that preceded the outcry, and without considering the reporting person as a possible perpetrator.

In each case, the child's behaviors and statements were critically important in ultimately determining whether or not the children were abused and, if so, by whom.   Observing the child with each parent or significant adult and obtaining a history from each provided an essential context for interpreting the child's behaviors and statements.

6

Children Speak Through Metaphors, Stories, and Drawings

Children speak through metaphors, stories, and drawings to say what they cannot say directly about their experiences with important persons in their lives. The events or participants may be too powerful for a child to confront in more direct language or deed.

If abuse has occurred, the child may fear the consequences to self or others of revealing feelings and experiences. The child may fear punishment or reprisal for disclosure or may fear that the abuser will be punished. Conflicted feelings and empathy for the abusive parent may prevent the child from disclosing the abuse in a direct way.

If abuse has not occurred, the child's wish to please each parent may lead the child to give answers to directed questions that indicate the other parent sexually abused the child. When this occurs, the child feels compelled to give "expected" answers in order to avoid getting into trouble.

A frequent recourse for the child is to use metaphors, stories, or drawings to communicate actual experiences. This chapter provides illustrative examples of those children's communications that, when interpreted correctly and in context, are vividly fluent and informative.

"MONSTERS HAVE LIVES TOO"

A conversation in an interactional assessment between 9-year-old Judy and 3-year-old Katie illustrates the older child's conflicted feelings about the stepfather who abused her and her little sister:

> *Katie.* Monsters are back, monsters, see the monsters and say "r-r-r-" to them and scare them away. Could you scare them away? Could you scare them away, Judy? Could you scare those monsters away? Could you talk to them?
>
> *Judy.* (*yawns, with no response*)
>
> *Katie.* Why don't you get those monsters?
>
> *Judy.* Because they have lives too and if like, if I went up to you and hit you, you wouldn't like that, want me to hit you real hard so you start crying? You don't want that, do you?
>
> *Katie.* Could you hit them?
>
> *Judy.* No.
>
> *Katie.* I will hit them.
>
> *Judy.* No, you don't want to hit them, because like if I came up to you and I hit you would you be sad.
>
> *Katie.* But the monsters are gone.
>
> *Judy.* No, don't open anything, you still don't want to hit anything.

Not only is Judy unwilling to help her little sister scare away the monsters, but also she attempts to get her sister to put herself in the position of the "monster" and to recognize that he has feelings, too. The statements "Because they have lives too," and "No, don't open anything," capture Judy's wish to keep the abuse secret in order not to disrupt the lives of others, even that of the monster. Katie acts without the support of Judy. She alone must get rid of the monsters.

Judy's conflicted feelings about her stepfather were expressed in a story she told about a wolf:

> There was a story about this kid and his wolf he had to take care of. These people killed it and they were saying all this stuff about him, like he was a mean wolf, he killed people. He was like a pet, he didn't do anything. They said his eyes were red and glared, real evil and this little boy that took care of it tried to say, "No, no, it's not, it was my pet." They didn't listen, they kept telling people lies about it, that it was mean, but the little kid was the only one that was right.

In her story the little boy who knew the wolf as a pet did not see the wolf as "evil" and "mean." The wolf has shown a tender side of himself to the little boy who cared for him, a side that others who had different experiences with him could not see.

Judy's response to a question about what kind of animal she would like to be demonstrated her vulnerability as a child completely dependent on others for care.

> Not a dog, because people beat you up and kick you. Not a cat because you get thrown out of the house. If you were a mean dog, you wouldn't like to be chained up. Not a bird because when you're young you might fall out of the nest. Not a fish, because you might be eaten.

She described all the bad things that happen to animals who rely on others for care as an allusion for her own predicament as an abused child.

Judy also used an animal metaphor to describe the difficulty a child has in getting adults to listen and to understand:

> I have rules, lots of things, opportunities. If you're a dog you sure don't get listened to. "Stop barking. What are you telling us. Stop barking. I'll answer your question if you talk human."

Mother's description of Judy's behaviors and statements beginning at age 3 confirmed that Judy's repeated efforts to tell someone about the abuse had met with failure. She recalled that when Judy was little she would tell Mother she had things to tell her. She described her response to Judy: "I would say you have to tell me. If you don't tell me, I can't help you." When Judy was 5, Judy told her teacher she had a secret.

The teacher conveyed concerns to Mother about something being wrong at home. Mother recalled that she ignored the teacher's concerns because she could not imagine what Judy would have a secret about. When Judy was 8 years old, Mother remembered Judy's prayers each night that she would die:

> Maybe that should have said to me something's not right, an 8-year-old who prays to God every night to take her life. Something's wrong and I should have been able to take her for help.

She recalled that when they moved to a new house, Judy was upset because she did not have a lock on the bedroom door. Not many months prior to the assessment, Mother had awakened and heard Judy's bed hitting the bedroom wall. She described her failure to respond either that night or the next day:

I was so tired and so deep in sleep that I couldn't get up. The next morning I didn't talk with her about it because I didn't want to believe that it could be. It couldn't possibly be.

As Mother described all the signals she had missed, Judy brought a picture of the peace symbol to mother (see Figure 1). This may have been her way of telling Mother that she was not angry with her for not being able to hear her. She understood Mother's conflicted feelings and her need to deny that anything was wrong.

"THERE'S A PAIR OF GLOVES THAT I NEED"

Nine-year-old Stewart's preoccupation with things being put in his mouth was observed throughout the session with his father, 10-year-old brother Jim, and 4-year-old sister Susie. It was as though he were trying to communicate to Father that he had clear memories of things Father might hope he had forgotten. A strange exchange occurred between Stewart and his father when the family was left alone for snack. Stewart asked Father to close his eyes and to open his mouth. Father refused to open his mouth until Stewart told him what he intended to do.

Father was settled in his career when Stewart was born and had more time to spend with the boys while their mother was out. He reported that he would "play a lot of floor play" with the boys. The play on words was interesting, although there was nothing explicitly sexual in his description.

Later in the interview, Father recalled the first smiles of the boys. He remembered Jim responded to touch and smiled a lot as a little baby. With Stewart, he could not remember smiles as early but remembered that they were "really big smiles." Perhaps recalling his own pleasurable experiences with Stewart, he

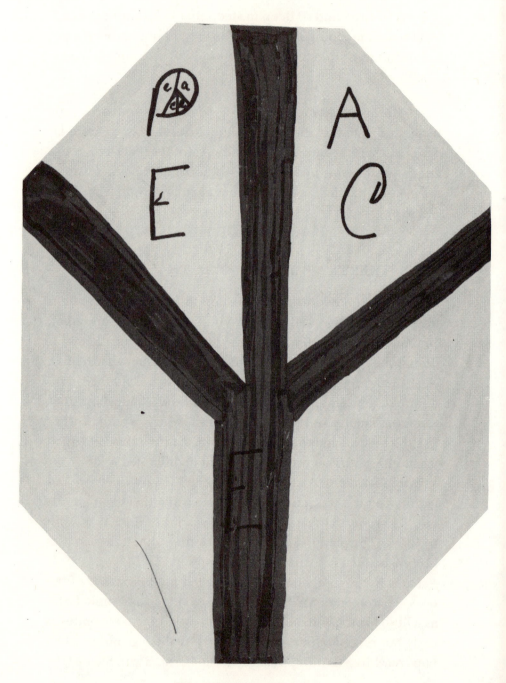

Figure 1. Peace Symbol

stated that Stewart was "a lot of fun; it didn't take a lot of stimulus because he was breastfeeding, so he was sensitive to that, a lot of touching." What is hinted at but not said suggests that whatever helped Stewart to nurse also enabled him to transfer this behavior to something else without a lot of stimulus.

After Father finished describing Stewart as a baby, Stewart reminded him of one thing he had forgotten to say: "Another thing, I always put things in my mouth." Father did not ask Stewart what he meant but immediately deflected attention from what Stewart had said by joking that Stewart used to want to eat frogs.

Stewart had learned to play extortion, distortion, and word games well. To make the threat of disclosure real, he needed to make sure Father knew he remembered the sexual games when he was little and also knew what happened to now 4-year-old Susie.

While having lunch with Father and her brothers, Susie asked Father, "Why do you hurt me?" to which Father responded, "I didn't—How did I hurt you?" Susie's answer was direct and clear: "With you." Her words suggest that Father hurt her with part of his body. Father's denial of hurting her was followed by his asking her where this had happened. Before Susie could answer, Stewart supplied the name of the town. After a quick glance to Stewart, Father assured Susie, "If you think about that real good, Daddy never ever hurt you honey, never ever."

The message that there were benefits to be derived from keeping the secret was not lost on Stewart, who immediately put in a request: "There's a pair of leather gloves I need." The cost to Stewart of keeping the secret was high. He almost choked on his hamburger as he repeated his request for the gloves when Father did not hear him. He had learned the rules of the game: he was using the threat of disclosure to manipulate Father just as Father used bribes to maintain his silence.

LEARNING THE FAMILY SCRIPT

Twelve-year-old Melissa provides insight into the price children pay for keeping the abuse secret. Her 9-year-old brother John, who disclosed physical and sexual abuse by their mother and stepfather, was in residential care. Melissa, who remained silent about the abuse, had been accepted back into the family and was living at home. When asked to describe John, each family member indicated characteristics that clearly conveyed he would have to recant if he wanted to become a part of the family once again.

Mother described him as "confused" and emphasized the loss of family as a consequence of disclosure:

> Very loving, very confused, lost, feeling of not belonging, sense of not knowing where he belongs, doesn't know who his family is, where his family is.

Stepfather focused on John's disclosure as not being truthful, and he conveyed the message that if John recanted he could "share with the family" in a different way than at present:

> A confused boy, I don't think he's nearly as confused now as he was a few years ago. I think he's made a lot of progress. Some people think he hasn't. I can tell the difference. Maybe it's a difference in myself. I don't know. I think John is a loving boy, a sharing boy, but he hasn't had time to share with the family. I think he's truthful. I don't think he was truthful at first.

Melissa supported her mother's and stepfather's perspectives in suggesting that John's disclosure had been untruthful and encouraging him to recant if he wanted to come home:

> I think this whole matter about John stinks. When a kid
> lies at first and they don't believe him, but when he's tell-
> ing the truth and they still don't believe him. That really
> stinks. You gotta believe a kid when he's telling you some-
> thing that's the truth or a kid's not gonna get nowhere at
> all. He's just gonna stay in the same place and never be
> able to come home. So I just think it stinks and he's a good
> boy too.

In her individual session, Melissa's response to a picture in
the Thematic Apperception Test (TAT) expressed not only her
concerns about her brother, but also the emotional cost to her
of keeping the secret:

> He is like depressed because he is having trouble playing,
> figuring out the song on his violin. He's looking for the
> violin and the script and thinking about how he can play it.

An implicit message was the high emotional cost of "figuring
out the family song." She was finding it more and more difficult
to play the family song and maintain any sense of integrity.

The cost to her of "playing...the song" to gain acceptance by
her mother and stepfather was expressed metaphorically in her
account of what she would have to do to fit in with friends at
school. She said that girls at school never chose her to participate with them in activities. When they did choose her, she always told them "no" because she liked to be by herself. She
described her current dilemma: if she said "yes" she would not
be by herself, but then she would have to do what they want.
She described how the girls argued, saying they did not like this
person and did not want her to be friends with the one she wanted
to be friends with. If she were friends with that person, they

would call her a traitor. To join her brother John in disclosure, she would risk being perceived as a "traitor," who would be rejected by her mother and stepfather. Like her brother, she would have no family at all.

The desperation Melissa felt was reflected in her play in the assessment with a doll who represented an ill child. She said the child was almost in a coma and needed immediate medical attention if she were to have any hope of recovery. She thought the *cops* should be called and the child put in foster care at once. When asked if children in foster care go back to their parents, Melissa replied, "Some do, it depends." In response to what the parents needed to do, she stated they needed to learn to take care of children. She thought they could probably learn this if they wanted to. She stated that sometimes parents were stubborn and could not learn to care for their children. When asked what should happen to the children of such stubborn parents, she responded,

> Give them a warning. If they don't get the baby help, put the baby in foster care and put her up for adoption if the parents don't stop being stubborn because the baby could die if she doesn't get help.

When asked how much time the parents should be given to stop being stubborn, she responded:

> The rest of the day. Twenty-four hours, plus bring the baby in and let us check her. We will decide about the parents.

The status of the child was the only reliable measure of whether the parents were no longer stubborn.

Melissa behaviorally demonstrated that both the girl and the boy needed to be checked for signs of sexual abuse. She stated she needed to check the girl doll's temperature and placed the thermometer in the crotch of the doll. She said the little girl had a temperature and was in danger of going into a coma unless immediately taken to hospital and given oxygen. When asked how the baby was feeling, Melissa said, "She can't talk, remember?" She then placed the thermometer in the boy doll's anus to check his temperature.

Melissa described a bleak picture of uncaring parents. She talked about fathers who drink and hurt children and about mothers who have babies but don't care about them. The following words reflect her sadness in never having parents who loved and cared for her:

> Parents have to care about children. If they don't, they might as well give them up for adoption. What's the use of making a child die.

No one offered her hope of a family. She could not let go of the only family she had available to her. She could not risk rejection by her mother and stepfather without having some degree of confidence that she would find a family to love and to accept her. Her brother's history may have reinforced her belief that silence was preferred to speaking out about the abuse. Disclosure would lead to rejection and loss of family.

FATHER AS RESCUER AND PROTECTOR

Four-year-old Joey came home from a weekend visit with his father with a sore bottom. Mother asked him if his father had put anything into his bottom; Joey said Father put a spoon in his bottom. As Mother asked questions, Joey elaborated the story to include activities with paternal cousins, aunts, uncles, and his grandmother and also reported that the activities with Father took place in a *bear cave*. As the story expanded, Mother expressed her concern that others would have difficulty in accepting the validity of Joey's statements:

> I can't tell people what this child is coming up with like "Oh sure" (*dismissive gesture*). You have to believe the child. I have to believe it all or I don't believe any of it.

In one of Joey's first sessions, in which the investigator-therapist asked directed questions to which Joey gave *expected* answers, Joey provided critical information about his mother's confusion of fantasy and reality. He said that once he told his mother a dream and she thought it was in real life.

During his play interview, conducted as a part of the interactional assessment, Joey repeatedly tested the evaluator to ensure that they both understood what things were real and what things were make-believe. Almost immediately, Joey established the need to differentiate what was real and what was make-believe. As he pressed Play Doh into round flat shapes, he announced, "I'm making cookies that nobody can eat."

When asked directly what his father had done to him, Joey responded in a cryptic manner: "Something up my butt and up my cousin Brad's." Joey was unwilling to provide any more detail, saying it would take "a couple of days, a long couple of days to tell what happened." Interpreting this to mean that Joey must be uncomfortable with the topic, the evaluator asked what would make it easier for Joey to talk about what happened to him. Joey responded, "Talk about it like we always do at [my therapist's]." When the evaluator asked how he talked about it with his therapist, Joey answered, "Say the things that happened to me." Joey's words suggested that he needed to be asked questions that suggested the answer in order to provide any further detail.

Although Joey's responses to directed questions seemed to support the allegation of sexual abuse by his father, recurrent themes in his play showed a protective, nurturing father. He consistently portrayed his father as the one who rescued the little bear from various kinds of dangers. In his play, Father Bear was the nurturing parent whom the little bear could count on to get him out of trouble and keep him safe.

Joey pretended he was the little bear puppet while directing the evaluator's words and actions as the daddy bear: "Dad rescues the little bear who is falling." As if to make certain the evaluator understood, he pointed out, "My father is just like that father" as he pointed to the father-bear puppet in the evaluator's hand. Joey pretended the little bear was in deep water catching fish. He instructed the evaluator, "Father says 'Are you all right?'" and then answered for the little bear, "Sure, I'm always all right."

The father bear had to fight the girl giants: "There's another giant left, a girl one, let's go get our weapons." As he shot the girl giant in the bottom, he expressed his hope that Father would triumph over the giants: "Father Bear will win this time." Joey described the bad things the giants had done, and clearly disassociated himself from them: "Crunched houses, knocked over things, pulled people's hair, they've eaten people, but I haven't," and instructed the evaluator to pretend the good giant rescued him. Again he instructed the evaluator to pretend that the father bear had to save the baby bear from the bad giant. When the evaluator commented, "It's nice to have a father bear like that," Joey replied, "Yeh, my father's just like that father."

When the evaluator reminded Joey that in the previous evaluation session Joey had stated that his father had abused him, Joey responded, "And once my dad was here," as though to remind the evaluator of his father's position that the abuse had not occurred. The evaluator repeated, "Your dad was here yesterday. How was that?" Joey responded, "Fine," before elaborating,

"Grandma Margie was on a trip and gave me a hat. My dad gave it to me."

The evaluator reflected what seemed to be Joey's positive feelings about Dad: "Was it fun to see your dad yesterday?" Joey answered, "I missed him." His words and affect conveyed a genuine sense of loss of his father. He expressed his relief that he still had a place at his father's house: "All the things he gave me haven't got lost."

Joey's good relationship with his dad was directly observed during the session with his father. Joey's respect for Father and yet his comfort with him were apparent during a father-son talk toward the end of the evaluation series.

Father invited Joey, "Come here, I want to talk to you, ask you some questions." As if familiar with this format, Joey approached Father and stood at attention in front of him. To help establish a more equal relationship with his son for their father-son conversation, Father asked Joey to pull up a chair. Joey walked past the small chairs to pull up a chair the same size as Father's. After climbing into the chair, Joey got down and pulled it closer to Father.

Father waited for Joey to get settled before he asked, "Tell me about the bear cave story." As he had been with the evaluator in his play session, Joey was reluctant to share the story that had caused so much trouble in his family and replied, "Only a little." When Father asked, "Why only a little?" Joey responded, "Because it would take too long." Father did not press Joey but simply responded, "Would it?" and then accepted Joey's terms. "Okay, just tell me a little."

As though he did not know exactly how to begin and also needed to empower himself, Joey looked at his play knife on the nearby table, stating that his grandma had given it to him. Father gave permission for Joey to get the knife and helped him fasten it to his belt. Joey also put the raccoon hat on his head and put the play "teeth" his mother had bought him in Father's shirt pocket. As Joey settled in with his chair close to Father's, Father encouraged him to tell the story, saying, "I've heard a lot about this story and I want to hear it from you."

Father communicated his openness to hearing whatever Joey had to say. He was smiling rather than stern and shared cookies back and forth as he leaned forward to listen to Joey's soft speech. He did not challenge what Joey said and himself brought up specific statements Joey had made that would appear to be incriminating to Father.

Joey began the story by saying, "Once Aunt Bessie got on me." Father repeated this and then asked if this had something to do with the bear cave story. Joey answered that it did and then added, "You weren't there." Instead of using this to exonerate himself from any involvement in what had allegedly happened at the bear cave, Father repeated, "I wasn't there?" and then asked, "Aren't I the one you usually go with on excursions?" Joey agreed with this but then stated that that time Father was not there.

Father shared a cookie with Joey before once again asking him to tell him about the bear cave story. Joey went directly to the heart of the confusion:

> *Joey:*   A story I made up.
> *Dad:*   Did you make up a story about the bear cave? Tell me the story.
> *Joey:*   About everything.
> *Dad:*   Tell me. You used to make up stories. Is this another one?
> *Joey:*   One of my dreams. I'll tell it to you. I'll tell it to you. I dreamed we have weapons at the bear cave. The bear cave was bigger than this house. We had to fight it, use a lot of things, put it on its ears and hurted his eardrums.

Dad: Oh yeah? (*shares cookie with Joey*)

Joey: We had diggers to see if his heart was on. We were nice to the bear. I wanted to see if anything was wrong with his ears, and you wanted to see if anything was wrong with it.

Dad: I did. Was anything wrong with it?

Joey: No.

What is striking is Joey's portrayal of his concern and that of his father about the well-being of the bear. They wanted to know if the bear's ears and heart were all right.

Dad: A dream you had? Tell me more. The reason I know about it is I heard it from somebody else.

Joey: From my mom?

Dad: No, not from your mom. I heard it from somebody who heard it from your mom.

For the next several minutes Joey recalled fishing, hunting, and the good times he and his cousins had with Father at Father's ranch. Father listened and shared cookies for a few minutes before again bringing him back to the topic at hand and stating specifically what Joey had said he put in his bottom:

Dad: What concerned me was you said I stuck a spoon up your butt.

Joey: That was my story.

Dad: Part of your dream.

Joey: No, my story.

Dad: Part of your story? Did that happen at the bear cave?

Joey: Nods head (*affirmative*).

Dad: Did I ever do that?

Joey: (*nods*) In my story I made up.

Dad: Then a story. Did I ever do that in real life?

Joey: (*shakes head no*)

Dad: A part of your imagination?

Joey: Yeah.

Dad: When you told that story did you tell your mom?

Joey: (*reaches out to take part of Dad's cookie*)

Dad: Did you tell the story to Mom? Did she think it was a pretty good story? Did she think it was make-believe?

Joey: No, she thought it was in real life.

Dad: Why would she think that, son?

Joey: (*touches each arm of chair*) This one's higher than this one.

Dad: Let's not get off the story. Why would she think it was a real story? Did you tell her it was real?

Joey Unh huh (*negative, with emphasis*).

Dad: Making up a story, then. Did your mom help you make up the story?

Perhaps recognizing that Father may now need to be empowered as they talk about Mother's role in the current situation, Joey removes the hat from his head and places it on Father's head:

Joey: She said it, and I said it, she—I—she—I.

Dad: She kept repeating the story? I'm not surprised. Don't think anything about it. You've been a pretty good boy, though, while I haven't seen you.

Father left a few minutes later, and the evaluator returned to the room. Joey washed the play teeth Mother had bought him and commented that he needed them to be nice and sharp and shiny. He then said, "They're my real teeth." When the evaluator stated that he might like to have teeth like that, Joey acknowledged, "Only they're not my real teeth," and he opened his mouth to show his real teeth to the evaluator.

When Mother returned to the room, Joey approached and pushed the teeth into her mouth hard enough that Mother complained, "That hurt." Play themes in the few minutes Joey was with his mother continued to portray Father as rescuer and nurturing parent. Joey also seemed to know that Mother's relationship with Father was unresolved, as he declared, "Our favorite man left, huh?" When Mother asked "What did you say?" Joey demanded a response as he loudly repeated his statement and ended with the word "Huh?"

EMBEDDED THEMES IN DRAWINGS

Children also express through drawings experiences that they may not be able to articulate in words. In cases of alleged sexual abuse, children may use drawings as a medium of expression when their words are misunderstood or when they fear the consequences of disclosure.

Accurate interpretation of a child's drawings depends on the evaluator's adherence to a few basic guidelines. Drawings are always interpreted within the context of other information. The child's age and developmental level must always be considered in interpreting drawings. Meaning may change depending upon this information. One also needs to know whether the child drew the picture with or without adult participation, the context in which it was drawn, and what the child said about the picture.

Sometimes drawings attributed to a child may not be those of the child. As Di Leo (1983) points out, "At first glance and without prior information one may be misled into attributing to a child the drawings by a psychotic adult" (p. 189). If, as Di Leo explains, drawings are "telling more about the subject than about the object drawn," then it is essential to accurately identify the person who drew the picture. For more information about interpretation of drawings, the reader is referred to Di Leo, (1983), Furth (1988), and Kellogg (1970).

Joey's Drawings

Drawings attributed to Joey between the ages of 4 and 6 depicted explicit sexual activities with his father and paternal relatives that on the surface appeared to substantiate the allegations that Father sexually abused Joey (see Figures 2, 3, and 4). These drawings were a part of over 300 drawings collected by Mother during a two-year period following Father's being awarded custody of Joey when the court found the allegations brought by Mother to be mistaken.

Stereotypic features suggestive of tracing, features and detail beyond the developmental level of Joey, and changes in positioning of the figures that occurred over time that were suggestive of vaginal rather than anal intercourse raised questions about the authenticity of the drawings. The drawings were, however, compelling enough that the court ordered a new series of evaluations of Joey and his parents that was to include among other things drawings by Joey in the presence of the examining psychologist.

The series of drawings in response to specific topics (Burgess & Hartman, 1993) given to him by the psychologist revealed Joey's perceptions and experiences related to his parents' divorce and the current situation. When asked to draw a picture of himself when he was younger, Joey drew a picture of himself in diapers (see Figure 5). In commenting on the picture, Joey said it was himself when he was a one-year-old, and that he was thirsty and wanted a drink of water. He was one year of age when his parents divorced.

He had difficulty when asked to draw a picture of his family. He first drew friends at school and identified himself as the one

Figure 2. "Dad Hurting Me" (age 5)

Figure 3. "Dad Hurting Me" (age 6)

Figure 4. "Dad Putting Penis in My Butt. Grandma Putting Knife Up My Cousin's Butt" (age 6)

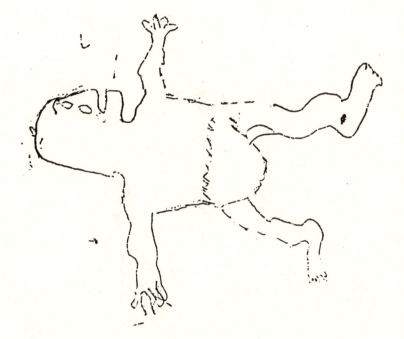

Figure 5. Whole Self When Younger (age 6 1/2)

Figure 6. Friends at School, Family #1

tilted to the right with his feet less solid than those of the others (see Figure 6). Note the prominent ears on Joey and on one of his friends. The second family picture was Joey with paternal cousins waiting in line to wrestle with Father, and the third was Joey with maternal cousins playing with "fake" arrows (see Figures 7 and 8).

Note the absence of feet in the picture of maternal cousins, while he and paternal cousins all have very solid footing, as if they are perhaps more grounded in reality.

When asked to draw what happened that caused the trouble in his family, Joey drew his mother and father standing in front of the judge (see Figure 9). Joey explained that the judge was with his mother and father, and that his father was the one on the left and his mother the one on the right. They were talking to the judge, who would have to decide where Joey would live.

When the evaluator asked Joey if he could just tell him what happened that caused the trouble in his family, Joey explained that he went to visit his father and came home with a sore bottom. His mother asked him if his father did anything, and he said yes. He then elaborated: "I said those things and I drew those pictures because I was scared, but my dad didn't do anything and I didn't want trouble for my dad, but I didn't want trouble for my mom and I was scared."

At the end of the session, Joey was asked to draw whatever he liked. He drew a picture of a cowboy with a horse (see Figure 10). He explained that this was a picture of himself as a cowboy with his horse, Blackie. There is a weed and a cactus in the picture, and his horse is eating a carrot. His airplane is in the sky. He said that when he grew up he wanted to be a cowboy and a pilot like his dad. He didn't know where this was and did not care as long as he could be a cowboy and pilot like his dad.

The missing features in this picture are instructive. The cowboy has no ears, although ears are present in other pictures of

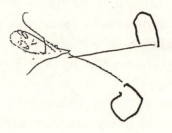

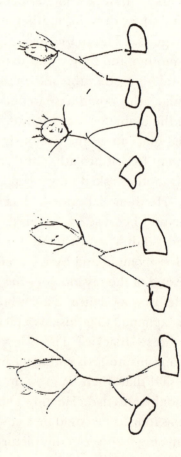

Figure 7. Waiting to Wrestle with Dad, Family #2

Figure 8. Maternal Cousins with Fake Arrows, Family #3

Figure 9. The Judge Will Decide

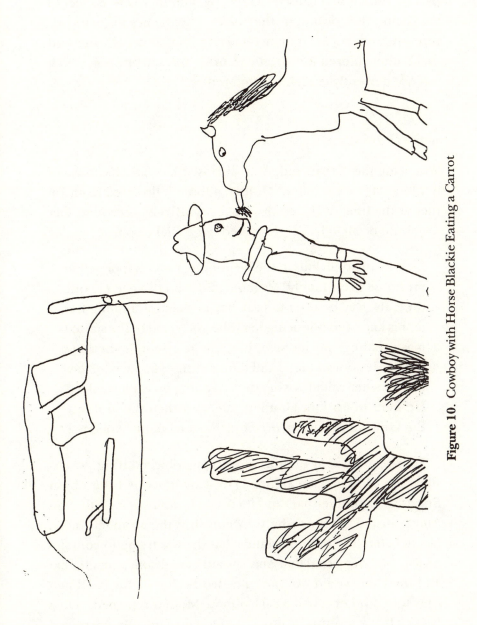

Figure 10. Cowboy with Horse Blackie Eating a Carrot

Joey in the series. The airplane and horse have no *bottoms* (the part of himself that caused the *trouble*), and there are no feet to the cactus, the cowboy, or the horse. The themes in Joey's pictures showed that his trauma related to his parents' divorce and that Father offered him safety, security, and nurturance, which was not currently available from Mother.

Amy's Drawing

When she was 3 years old, Amy disclosed her father's abuse of her to a day-care teacher. Mother, although divorced from Father at the time of the disclosure, had difficulty accepting that the abuse occurred. She described her initial response:

> I was a little oblivious in the beginning, never happened in my house to my family. My mom said something to me one time, the way he used to rock her to sleep, straddling her on his knee and bouncing her. She got to where she started masturbating. My mom said I think he's doing something to her. It floored me. I still didn't want to know. The day-care teacher called, saying she was going up against tables. He went to work in another state, and she calmed down. But I still didn't put it in my mind that something happened.

Four-year-old Amy drew a large oblong object during the session with Mother (see Figure 11). Amy described the object first as a "big poofer hat" and then said it was a rock. Although Amy enlisted Mother's help in coloring the strange object, Mother still did not understand what she was trying to communicate. She suggested that Amy should have drawn a smaller hat and then she would not have needed help to color it. When Amy told mother it had a rock on top, Mother repeated, "Oh a rock? It's a mountain now?" Amy emphatically corrected

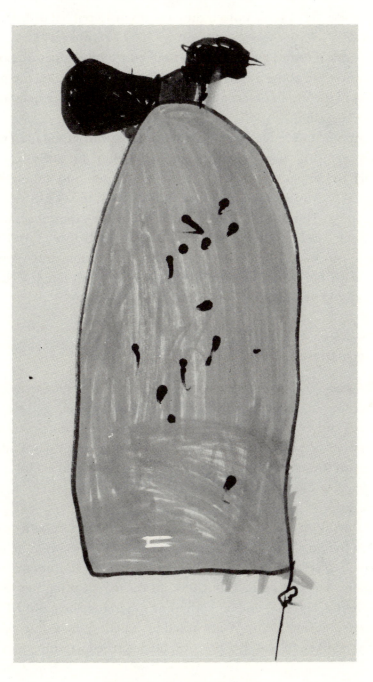

Figure 11. "Big Poofer Hat"

Mother: "It's a rock, not a mountain, it's just a big hat with a ball on it."

A few minutes later as Mother talked to the evaluator about wanting the abuse gone from Amy's mind, Amy folded the picture of the green object and took it to Mother, telling her, "You can keep that."

Amy's knowledge of a penis that gets big with stimulation was apparent in a play interview conducted after the sessions with each of her parents. She positioned her fingers and thumb as if encircling something and asked the evaluator to keep the water running. Her words are informative about her experiences with Father: "Before I turn it real fat, it will be hot, before I turn it so big." She said, "I can't get it on my hand," and afterwards wanted to wash her hands because they were "dirty," although clearly she had been holding her hand under the water.

Julie's Drawing

Six-year-old Julie drew a picture of a horse in response to her therapist's request to tell him about her mother's alleged sexual abuse of her (see Figure 12). Two years earlier, Julie described unusual behaviors of her stepfather. She reported that Poppa put his fingers in her *pee pee* and in her *pooh*, would *eat* her pee pee, and that his fingers smelled bad when he put them in her mouth.

During an interview with law enforcement, the stepfather said that Julie had grabbed his penis a couple of times when he was toweling off after a shower. Each time he asked her not to do it again. He said he had touched her during cleaning her after toileting, and that one time when he wiped her she grabbed his hand and smelled it. When asked to explain Julie's statements that he liked to "eat" her pee pee, he described wrestling play in

Figure 12. "Babies Can't Talk"

which he put his mouth on her stomach and blew or bit her on the rear in a playful manner.

Despite Julie's clear verbal statements of abuse by the stepfather, the allegations were not substantiated with respect to the stepfather. Over the next two years, professionals involved in the case began to see the stepfather as the more adequate parent and to suspect that the mother had sexually abused Julie. In a session with her therapist, who was questioning Julie about what Mother had done, Julie again tried to say that the one who hurt her had a penis. Julie responded to her therapist's question by saying, "Babies can't talk." She conveyed in her picture what she could not say in words. The head of the horse bears a striking resemblance to a penis. The face has puffed out cheeks, perhaps suggesting her experience of oral sex with her stepfather.

Roger's Drawings

Nine-year-old Roger's difficulty in telling about the abuse by his stepfather is seen in a series of pictures he drew when asked to draw his family. He was involved in the evaluation because of allegations that his 2-year-old stepsister had been sexually abused by her father. His mother and stepfather were divorced at the time of the evaluation, and no one suspected the boy had also been abused.

His mother said Roger was a good artist, and indeed his pictures show some artistic talent. Yet he could not draw his family without sexual themes intruding into the picture. He kept starting and stopping and starting again on a new piece of paper (see Figures 13, 14, and 15). Roger's pictures were suggestive of

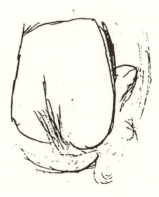

Figure 13. Family Drawing #1

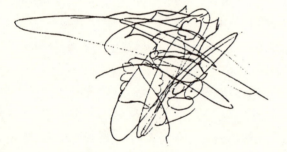

Figure 14. Family Drawing #2

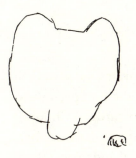

Figure 15. Family Drawing #3

sexual activities with a male perpetrator. One can speculate that the perpetrator exercised control over Roger that allowed the abuse to go on over a period of time and that secured his silence even after his mother's divorce from the stepfather.

CONCLUSION

The material presented in this chapter illustrates the variety of ways in which children tell adults about their experiences, whether positive or negative, abusive or nurturing. Children who have the capacity for speech often cannot disclose their feelings and experiences in the way adults need and expect them to. They may be afraid; they may fear being misunderstood; they may feel sympathy for the one who hurt them.

A myriad of reasons may prevent them from being able to say in a straightforward way what they must communicate if they are to be assured of being loved and cared for and kept safe from harm. Stories, metaphors, and drawings often provide the only channel for them to safely explore and communicate confusing and traumatic events or to express positive feelings and experiences with a parent mistakenly accused of abusing them.

7

Children Speak Through Behavioral Reenactments

The two case illustrations in this chapter demonstrate how children express their feelings and disclose confusing and traumatic experiences through behavioral reenactments (Schetky, 1991). A child's behaviors are often dramatic and graphic. Although interpretation of the child's behaviors depends on what is known about the incident from other sources, the behaviors may also illuminate what otherwise has been obscure.

In the Kempe Interactional Assessment for Parent-Child Sexual Abuse, play materials are much more than aids to assist the child's verbal communication or to enable the child to physically demonstrate what has occurred. They are the medium through which a child can express the full range of conscious and unconscious emotions and reenact significant experiences. The child's reenactment may not be, nor should an evaluator expect it to be, an exact duplication of the events. It does, however, capture and convey the child's perceptions and experiences associated with the event.

LAURA'S OUTCRY

A live-in baby-sitter reported the abuse of 2-and-1/2-year-old Laura and her younger sister. The baby-sitter had suspected the abuse from abundant and undisguised activity in the family home after being in the home for only a week and a half; her suspicion was confirmed when she walked into the bathroom to find Laura and her father nude. Father's penis was in Laura's mouth.

Father denied the baby-sitter's allegations, claiming that the baby-sitter wanted "revenge" against him for not paying her and was obtaining that revenge by separating him from his family. Mother not only supported Father's denial but countered with a claim that the baby-sitter had abused Laura. With no observable display of emotion, Mother calmly acknowledged all of the signs of abuse contained in the baby-sitter's letter to authorities as things she herself had observed but portrayed them as proof of abuse by the baby-sitter.

Both parents grew up in dysfunctional families, and each brought pathologic influences from their own childhood experiences into their new family. Mother characterized herself as a different kind of mother to her children than her own mother had been to her but, as her own mother had done, "picked her men" over her children:

> I'm not an excessive drinker, I don't beat my children, I'd never turn my back on them. I came from a very different background. My father died when I was 7 years old. Mother had me for a while. I've been in foster care, I lived in eight different foster homes on two different occasions. My mother always picked her men over me, she never stood up for us kids.

Father identified with his stern stepfather and recreated in his family the same atmosphere of fear he and his mother had experienced:

I'd like to raise my kids. My parents never raised me. My grandparents raised me...my folks separated when I was 5. I didn't get along with my stepfather. It was easier to live with my grandparents...[my stepfather's] sternness. I never quite could measure up to what he expected. She always took his side. He could be stern with her too. There was like no escape.

From the moment Laura entered the assessment play room, she engaged in determined and deliberate activity to communicate with the evaluator what had happened to her with Father. She had very little verbal language, however, to express her experiences, and used nonverbal gestures and behaviors to reenact experiences with Father. Each successful communication led to another.

Her first series of actions communicated an association with the bathroom, an oblong object, and being hurt. She picked up and put down the toy duck (bathroom toy), removed the rings from the pole and showed the pole to the evaluator, and then showed the evaluator her finger while expressing hurt. She demonstrated that things had been put in her mouth: she pushed the doll bottle into the doll's mouth, her mouth, and then extended it toward the evaluator's mouth.

As the session continued, Laura worked to help the evaluator understand her experiences with Father. She pointed to the long, narrow microphone that extended about 10 inches from the ceiling. This was followed by an attempt to undress the small adult male doll-figure in the dollhouse. To help Laura accomplish what she was attempting with that doll, the evaluator said, "The clothes on these dolls (reference to small doll-figures) don't come off, but those dolls' clothes can come off" (reference to the anatomically correct dolls).

Laura immediately abandoned the small adult male doll-figure to undress the adult male anatomical doll. She removed the adult male doll's shirt. After pulling the pants partially down, she gave the adult male doll to the evaluator and pulled at the pants with attention to the evaluator as though requesting her help in removing the pants. As the evaluator pulled the pants down past the penis, Laura touched it, then grabbed and squeezed it. With attention to the evaluator, she made an "agh" sound. This sound was heard again and again in connection with toys or actions associated with Daddy and the bathroom.

Leaving the adult male doll with the evaluator to finish undressing, she turned to a little girl doll and removed its panties. She gave the little girl doll to the evaluator and signalled a request for help to remove the doll's dress. With the adult male doll and little girl dolls nude, Laura pushed the doll bottle into the little girl doll's mouth. This was followed by inserting her index finger into the little girl doll's mouth. With a whimpering sound she extended her finger to the evaluator.

Over and over again she repeated these actions that showed a connection between something inserted into the little girl's mouth and pain to the little girl. She communicated a sense of coercion and aggression toward the little girl as she shoved the doll bottle hard into the little girl doll's mouth and then forcefully pulled the ribbon attached to the doll's head.

Even when Laura was able to turn to other activities, she remained hypervigilant to adult male voices from outside the room. While coloring with the crayons, she responded to a male voice with, "Daddy?" then resumed coloring but quickly interrupted her coloring to push the bottle into the little baby doll's mouth. She pointed to various parts of the doll's body while making whimpering sounds. The evaluator redirected Laura's attention to the anatomical dolls and asked if she wanted to show her anything else with the dolls. Laura picked up the male doll and squeezed his penis. Simultaneously with this action, Laura puffed out her cheeks and with attention to the evaluator opened and closed her mouth making an "agh" sound.

Laura spontaneously searched out other toys in the room that helped her to graphically express to the evaluator what happened to her and her feelings about her experiences. Laura walked across the room to the monkey and alligator puppets in the chair. She gave the puppets to the evaluator. She used the alligator, whose mouth had a zipper in it, to show things being forced into the mouth. This time, however, the zipper gave her control over whether the mouth was open or closed. She would open the mouth, insert her finger, and make a gagging "agh" sound before zipping it shut and firmly pressing her own lips together.

Through her behavior, Laura clearly demonstrated what had happened to her and how she had experienced it. When she felt her communications had been understood, Laura gathered into her arms two baby dolls and walked to the door of the assessment room with them to leave; she had been successful.

This case illustrates how a child's communications through behavioral reenactments confirm and are confirmed by information from parents or others about the events the child has experienced. Laura unequivocally reenacted in her play with dolls, animals, and other materials during the session what the baby-sitter had described. Laura's play corroborated the baby-sitter's story of finding Father and Laura nude in the bathroom with Father's penis in Laura's mouth.

With the aid of videotapes of Laura's play session and the parents' interactions with the children in the assessment, the children were adjudicated as dependent and neglected. In a concurrent criminal matter, Father pled guilty to sexual abuse of the children and was sentenced to 12 years in state prison. Parental rights were terminated for Father at the time of his sentencing and for Mother almost two years later when she was unable to repair her relationship with her children and to demonstrate her ability to provide minimally adequate parental care for them.

THINGS THAT GO BUMP IN THE NIGHT

Susie at age 4 had good language abilities, but her repeated requests to a male evaluator to play "daddy and the baby" and for
the male evaluator to be the daddy had not been satisfied. Despite the fact that her only verbal disclosure had been limited, at
age 3, when she had told an examining physician that her daddy
had hurt her, the evaluator expected that Susie could now articulate to him in words experiences she had with Father before
she was 3. But for Susie, despite a year in therapy, what her
father had done to her was still too traumatic and confusing for
words; she needed to express her experience in behavior before
she would be able to express her experience in words.

In her play interview Susie repeatedly told the evaluator that
she wanted to play "daddy and the baby." He did not see the
relevance of this and continued to encourage Susie to tell him
what happened with Daddy. Toward the end of her play interview, Susie placed her hands over her ears and in a loud tone of
voice said, "You can't hear me. I can't hear you." She was giving
a clear message that they were not communicating. The evaluator continued to encourage Susie to tell him what happened
with Daddy. Susie again requested, "Let's play babies. You're
the daddy."

Susie placed her hands over her ears and said, "I'm not going
to talk. You won't make me. I won't." Susie then walked to the
door and left the room, saying, "I'm not playing anymore." The
evaluator said he would stop asking questions and she could draw
or do what she liked. Susie stuck her head in the door and
announced the conditions on which she would agree to continue the session: "We're gonna play baby, and you're the daddy
this time."

When the evaluator acquiesced, Susie clearly demonstrated
the abuse that had occurred. She communicated that strange
things had happened with Daddy on many nights prior to the

night in which Father's actions finally led to her hysterical scream-ing. Susie pretended to have dinner and then pretended to go to sleep. In her play, the baby went to sleep first while the daddy was still eating dinner. There were sounds in the night that woke the baby. Each time the baby was reassured by someone that what was happening was normal and was told to go back to sleep.

With the evaluator, Susie lay on the table with her hands un-derneath her in her crotch simultaneously protecting and touch-ing herself; she lifted and lowered her legs while holding them in a stiff position as she made noises. When the evaluator asked what kept waking them up when they slept, Susie gave a differ-ent answer each time. She said it was only the trash can, the wind, the thunder, the clock, the train. With each explanation she would tell him to go back to sleep. Finally, Susie was able to move from noises made by things to noises made by a person. She said the trashman was making the noise and instructed the evaluator: "Yell out 'Don't do that, I'm trying to go to sleep.'"

Susie announced it was morning time and time to get up. They had to cook and then go back to sleep again because it was nighttime. Susie made another sound in the middle of the night. When the evaluator asked what it was, she said the baby just screams in the night. She got in bed with the baby doll and instructed the evaluator to go back to sleep.

Morning came again, followed by another night in which Susie continued to command him to go back to sleep when she made noises that woke him up. Susie instructed the evaluator to turn around and not to look while she changed the doll's diapers. It was then time to get "jammies" on and go to bed again. As she got closer to the scary part of what happened with Daddy, her anxiety increased. For a moment she seemed confused as she tried to put the doll clothes on herself instead of the doll.

Despite the evaluator's apparent failure to understand what Susie was telling him, she overcame other obstacles inadvert-ently placed in her way by the evaluator. When the evaluator interrupted her play to ask if it would be all right to have visits with her daddy, Susie told him, "Wait. I'm not finished." She lifted blankets off the baby's bed and exclaimed, "Got the blanket wet!" As she was about to pour water from the large nursing bottle onto the doll in the bed, the evaluator suggested that she should do this over the sink. Susie agreed and took the doll and bottle to the sink. When the evaluator suggested that they were almost done with the session, Susie emphatically said, "No we're not." Susie was determined to finish telling the evaluator what had happened with Daddy and the baby.

Susie squirted water from the bottle onto the doll's face. She said she had to dry the baby's face and then give it a bath. She sang as she washed the baby. She said that she had to wash the baby's hands and then put the baby back to bed. When the evaluator asked if she had anything else to tell him, Susie responded, "I need to tell you something else. We can visit with my daddy again too. You're a very good man." Now Susie was ready to have that visit with her daddy. She had told her story and was confident that the evaluator who had listened to her knew what happened to her.

Father, in the interview, tried to normalize Susie's communication of her experience but failed:

> I saw the children on [one weekend and] I missed the next time and saw them again [almost three weeks later]. Susie had been taken to the doctor three days previous to that visit and was reluctant to take her clothes off. She was quiet and didn't say anything. She appeared to be—well, you have the report. I picked them up for visitation. Nothing was told to me about the doctor. In the process of the visit, we play, have a good time (*clears throat*). In the middle of the night, she has a nightmare, wets the bed, standing in the——, I wake up and she's wailing in the bathtub in the bathroom. We had left the light on so she could go potty.

She has all her clothes off, wet from one end to the other. She was really upset. Previously pretty regular basis nightmares and wetting the bed....I'm informed she has a bed and she's worried about wetting the bed. No big deal. I have plastic on it. In the process I walked in, sat down, kneel down next to the bathtub, she was really upset, wake these guys up, come in, see what she is, get her dressed, get her back to bed, the next day, we play have a good time, ride bicycles, visit friends.

Susie did get a chance to visit her father again. It was during lunch with him after her play session and without any intervening contact with her mother and stepfather. Within minutes of her reunion with father and in the presence of her two brothers, Stewart and Jim, she looked at her father and asked, "Why did you hurt me?" Father denied he would ever hurt his Susie. When he asked where he had hurt her, Stewart named the town where the incident occurred that had led to Susie's hysterical screaming in the middle of the night.

Protected contact with Father during the interactional assessment was therapeutic for Susie. Not only was she able to reenact what her father had done to her, but she also gained the courage and ability to tell her father in direct words that he had hurt her. When he asked, "How?" her simple and articulate response was "With you."

When information from the evaluation was made available to the court, Father chose to have no contact with any of his children rather than to acknowledge the abuse and enter into treatment.

CONCLUSION

Laura and Susie illustrate how children use behavioral reenactments to articulately communicate where, how, and when events happened with important persons in their lives. Often the most effective way to present the children's communications to a court is to simply present the videotaped record of the behavioral re-enactment with the evaluator acting as a translator.

8

Behavioral Clues to Experiences

Children and parents exhibit behaviors in the assessment observation and interview periods that provide accurate and vital clues
to the quality of their attachment relationships and that often
illustrate specific experiences they have shared. These behaviors verify the accuracy of other history and relationship information gathered in the assessment; they may directly and vividly
demonstrate the abusive nature of the relationships.

Children often exhibit learned or customary behaviors with each
parent and initiate activities that are a part of a familiar exchange
with the parent. If the relationship has involved sexual grooming or
sexual activities, the young child's behavior with this parent may
reflect these activities. Although the parent may believe or desire
that others will not understand the sexual content of the behaviors,
the parent may become an active participant rather than a passive
object of the behaviors. The evaluator must be alert for behaviors
that are symbolic repetitions of sexual activities.

"IN ME BOTTOM"

It was difficult to believe that the young father who looked so boyish could have sodomized his 4-and-1/2-month-old son Sean—despite clear physical trauma consistent with anal penetration. It was equally difficult to believe that a mother who had been home during the time of the alleged abuse could have ignored the screams of her baby or be complicit with her husband. The couple also had a 2-year-old girl, Kristy. Both children had been removed from the home upon discovery of the injury to Sean.

The mother and father both asserted that Sean's injuries were not the result of sexual abuse. Rather, as they described it, the incident occurred in the early hours of the morning. Mother stated she had fed and diapered Sean and then placed him on a blanket on the floor in the bedroom. She could not sleep and went to watch television in the next room.

Father reported that he was getting dressed for work when he noticed it had snowed overnight. The clothes he needed were stored in a duffel bag in the closet. He gave the following account of what happened:

> I was taking it down when I dropped it. I don't know where
> it hit, it hit him on his lower section. Sean was underneath
> it, so I picked it up.

When asked to clarify where this occurred, Father replied, "Underneath me on a blanket." Father then explained that Sean was on the floor in the bedroom and must have crawled into the closet. Mother, as if aware that the story was not holding together, explained, "It's hard to know exactly where he is. Sean's always been very mobile even when he was very very young." Sean was 4-and-1/2-months old at the time of the incident, and now at 6 months he was barely mobile.

Mother reported that the "split between the scrotum and the anus" could have occurred with the impact. She added that the doctors also said the "anal sphincter was stretched" and that this could have happened "if something on the surface of the bag stuck out of it." When the evaluator asked if there were anything in the bag that stuck out, Mother shrugged and Father shifted his feet. The question was repeated and Father answered, "No, certain things they stick out, but I didn't have them in there at the time."

The subject of injuries to Sean was broached again when the evaluator asked who had noticed the bruises first. Father immediately said, "She did." Mother said, "Yes, but we were not in the room together." Father then elaborated:

> She took the diaper off, after I took the duffel bag off of him. Thought it knocked the wind out of him. He didn't cry, then started crying. He was ripping his diaper off. It took Kristy such a long time to take her diaper off, even pull it off. He was doing it. I was kind of like, I don't know, power. This little child has this much strength. [I was] going out to go show her [mother]. She took his diaper off. He had this big bruise on it, not like he was punched. Doctor didn't agree with it. It would be just as possible for spot indentation between finger and stuff (*demonstrates closed hand with finger of other hand inserted in it*). I guess she noticed the bruise.

Mother explained, "I went into the room because Sean started crying." When asked how soon the bruise appeared after the bag was dropped on Sean, Father said, "About 30 seconds after, not long." Mother gave a different answer, one that contradicted her previous statement of going into the room because she heard Sean crying: "He came out. We talked for a second, probably a couple of minutes."

At this point in the interview, Mother and Father were briefly distracted by two-year-old Kristy, who while laying supine on the floor touched her anal area and said, "In me bottom." Father asked, "What's wrong with your bottom?" Mother repeated the question. Father repeated the question. Kristy answered, "No." Father asked, "No, what? Don't you start scratching your bottom." Mother laughed and said, "Okay," as if this took care of the problem.

Kristy's words and behavior gave a direct clue to how Sean had gotten the bruises, the tear, and the enlarged anal sphincter. To deflect attention from what Kristy had said, Mother quickly continued the interview with the comment that Sean's injuries might have been caused by an infection. She stated that she also had an infection when she was in the eighth grade. She distanced herself from any knowledge of what happened with Sean and Father in the other room by saying, "I didn't hear anything. I was in the other room and had the TV on."

An interaction between Kristy and her father with a string of pop beads was instructive about the kinds of activities engaged in at home and about the mother's attempts to deflect attention from signs of their unhealthy, atypical relationships. Kristy initiated a "game" in which she attached beads to a chain that Father held extended from his crotch. When Father flipped the chain and made a sucking sound, Kristy looked up at him and closed her mouth while puffing out her cheeks and making a sucking sound. With a quick downward glance to the pop beads in Father's crotch, she said "Boogie." Father complimented her: "Good girl."

Kristy named the colors of the beads as she attached them to the chain. When Kristy named an orange bead "blue," her father laughed and tickled her stomach with the bead chain. Kristy backed away. She then bent forward and grabbed her crotch. With her hand in her crotch, she said, "Get, get" and walked toward Father. Mother's comment acknowledged that she had been watching the game and knew the game would cause concern. She attempted to deflect attention from Father and Kristy by commenting, "Maybe she's color-blind." This feigned ignorance of what was occurring in front of her more accurately described Mother's "blindness" with respect to her husband's sexual abuse of both Sean and Kristy.

The evaluator then asked Father what he did with the children during visits with them; Father responded, "Basically I hold Sean and I play with Kristy." Ironically, he was accurately describing the sexualized activity he engaged in with each child throughout the assessment and Mother's complicity in them. The games with Kristy gave clues of more overt sexual activities that occurred at home. His interactions with Sean while holding him in the assessment recreated activities he enjoyed with Sean at home.

At the assessment reunion with Kristy and Sean, Mother ignored Sean, who was in the evaluator's arms, to pick up Kristy. She encouraged Father to take Sean, stating, "You know you like your daddy best." This preference for Father was not at all obvious during the next few minutes. Sean began to fuss almost immediately as Father sat with him in his lap. Father suggested that Sean wanted a hug from Mother. Father's lingering gaze as he handed Sean to Mother was more like the look of a lover than a father to his infant son. Mother gave Kristy to the father with the command, "Go give Daddy a hug, while I give the baby a kiss." Father embraced Kristy and gave her a lingering kiss to her mouth.

When Sean began to fuss again, Mother asked, "You want your bottle?" Although Father got up to get the bottle for Mother, she gave Sean to him to feed. Sean refused to allow Father to put the bottle into his mouth. He arched backward away from the bottle and turned his head to keep Father from inserting the nipple into his mouth. Sean's negative reaction to Father's efforts to feed escalated and his fussy vocalization turned to crying. As if aware of Sean's unusual behavior and perhaps knowing the meaning of this, Mother gave excuses for Sean's resistance to the father's feeding of him. Although Sean had had nothing to eat, Mother said he might need to burp. She wondered if he was "Mr. Grouchers" because he had to get up so early.

Father's reactions to Sean's unhappiness with what should have been mutually satisfying nurturing activities were informative. He held Sean to his shoulder, bounced him up and down, and asked the question, "Do you like this?" When this position did not produce the pleasure Father wanted, he shifted Sean to face away and bounced him up and down with Sean's feet hitting him in the crotch. This positioning seemed to please Father, who then said to Sean, "I'll hold you the way you like it."

When Sean continued to fuss and cry, Mother asked, "What's going on?" Father's answer on behalf of Sean was one that might be given for a spouse not in the mood for intimacy: "I have a headache." Mother repeated Father's words as if Sean had spoken, "You have a headache, son?"

As Father's bouncing of Sean became more vigorous, Father turned away from the camera before placing Sean on the floor. Father seated himself on the couch behind Sean and stared at his bottom. Father leaned forward, lifted Sean's shirt, and touched the side of his stomach. Even after he withdrew his hand, his attention remained focused on Sean's bottom. As if he were trying to control himself, Father covered his eyes, shook his head, clasped his hands together, and with his thumbs caressed his own hands. He glanced toward Mother and Kristy who were playing nearby. He commented that Sean was "getting a lot better." Mother who was involved with Kristy did not respond. Father resumed staring at Sean's bottom and then looked at his own crotch. He stood up, reached between his legs, and lifted and replaced the couch cushion. He positioned himself on the floor and hovered over Sean, supporting himself on his hands and knees in a recreation of the position in which Sean had been sodomized.

At a later point, Father attempted to put booties on Sean. Father's words to Sean, who resisted his efforts to put his booties on him, were suggestive:

> No, don't cry. You're still fighting me...he doesn't want them on. He's fighting me. Why are you fighting me? Let Daddy put on your bootie. I really don't want to hurt an ankle. Why are you pulling your feet away from me? I'm trying to tie it. You're being a bugger.

When Sean successfully pulled the bootie away, Father enthusiastically called Mother's attention to this. "Look what he did! He pulled it. He's pulling it away." His pleasure in Sean's action was similar to what he described when Sean pulled his diaper off the morning when the bruises were first noticed. At that time, he recalled calling to his wife to come see because he was so proud that Sean was strong enough to do this.

Mother's willingness to dismiss signs of Father's sexual deviance was expressed in her words, "It's just a bootie." As Father continued to struggle to get Sean's bootie on him, he commented, "You were so much easier before." Mother sympathized with Sean: "It's okay, son, you don't have to wear that nasty bootie."

Following the session in which the children were present, the evaluator suggested that others were saying the injuries resulted from sexual abuse. Mother nodded and reached over to pick up a string of pop beads from the floor. Father, who was already holding a string of pop beads, smiled and whispered, "That's my toy." This and subsequent actions gave the impression that the pop beads were a symbol of sexual addiction for both parents.

A few minutes later when each parent was asked what they would expect the other to do if they thought the other parent had sexually abused their children, Father responded, "I would expect her to leave me. How can you live with someone like that?" Mother confirmed this would be her response: "It would be like I didn't even know him if he did something like that, but like I know he wouldn't do that."

As if to symbolically get rid of the part of him that caused the trouble, Father tossed the string of pop beads to the other side of the couch. Mother continued to hold her beads for a few more minutes until the question about whether someone who did something like that could get help was directed to Father. After each had discarded their beads, they stared at the evaluator. It was as if they had nothing else important in their lives to hold onto, if they were to give up their sexual addictions.

When Father was asked if he thought that someone who did this could get help, he pulled his coat closer around him as he answered:

> I know the question is directed to me. I don't know, I'm not in a position, I don't care what anyone says.

His behavior showed that he would use the coping strategies he had used all his life. He would hide the abuse rather than acknowledge it and seek help. Father's response to the question about what he would like to change in his life showed that he would cover up his abusive behavior the next time:

> Not have gotten her [the mother] a ride to the hospital. I would probably have changed, not have gotten down the duffel bag right then (*laughs*). If I would have did this, I would have known the bruises were caused by it. Why did I ever get her a ride. I would have told my wife, "Oh this is caused by this. Okay, fine."

This response shows that he would have chosen a better time to abuse Sean and would have been prepared to offer more plausible explanations to his wife for the bruises. He had no remorse for what he did. He only had self-recrimination for not covering up better so that no one would have suspected sexual abuse.

Mother's response to the same question showed that she believed she also made a mistake in taking Sean to the doctor, because it had resulted in the loss of her babies:

> I don't know. I just want my babies back. Everything I do is for my kids. It is important for them to feel secure and for me to be there for them.

It is ironic that "being there" only meant physically being there. It did not include protecting them from being hurt.

Each parent adamantly denied a history of sexual abuse in his or her own childhood, although each described experiences of not being protected by their mothers, who had ignored or made excuses for a physically and emotionally abusive father. Father repeatedly alluded to a change in his relationship with his father because of events between the ages of 8 and 11. As he grew up, he learned to do whatever anyone required of him:

> Basically, I would do whatever anyone said, wanted me to do,...even if they were like school teachers, I said, "Okay." ...When I started getting older, I would do what my dad said or anybody; they must know better. I didn't want to get in trouble. (*laughs*)

Mother described her mother as a "wimp," and as a fairly unreliable person. She recalled her mother making excuses for her abusive stepfather:

He's sick is what my mom used to always say. My mom used to say, "He's sick. It's the result of diabetes," which it is, but that is no reason to take it out on me.

No criminal charges were filed in this case. Mother divorced Father and in this way distanced herself from him, but the children remained at risk. Although there was clear physical evidence of trauma to Sean consistent with sexual abuse, clinical information to show risk factors for both parents, and behavioral clues to sexual experiences for both Sean and Kristy, this information was not presented to the court.

"THAT NASTY OLE THING"

In the assessment, 14-month-old Celie repeatedly approached her father as he sat with legs crossed on the couch beside her mother. She pulled herself to a standing position by holding onto his legs, and then thrust her head into his crotch. This was followed by a twist of her body away while still holding onto his leg for support.

The stimuli that triggered this response was simply Father's sitting on the couch with one leg crossed over the other knee or a touch to her face by either Mother or Father. Although Father occasionally ignored this behavior, he most often would lift Celie into his lap. In one instance in which he lifted her over his head, she threw her head back and, with a high-pitched laugh, pushed her hands against her father's head in an approach-avoidance kind of pattern.

Celie consistently refused when Mother offered her a bottle and struggled against Mother's efforts to feed her. When Celie refused to take the bottle from Mother, Mother said, "I know what you want." She placed the bottle in Father's crotch and placed Celie on the floor facing Father. Father looked away while he quickly removed the bottle from his crotch and placed it on the couch beside him.

Without any encouragement from Father, Celie crawled to Father, and when he picked her up, she dived into his crotch almost as if she expected the bottle to be there. Father placed her in a feeding position and was able to feed her briefly. Within minutes of Father's feeding her and while still in his arms, Celie began to gag and to spit up. Mother's words, "Did Daddy put that nasty ole thing in your mouth again?" suggested she knew what historically led to Celie's gagging. It was not always just the bottle that Celie found in her father's crotch.

The interview with the parents revealed that Celie's gagging and refusal of the bottle from her mother began at home when she started to crawl and pull herself up to the couch. The parents initially denied that Celie had ever gagged prior to being removed from their care; they also blamed "rotten milk" and someone deliberately trying to make them look bad for Celie's gagging and spitting up when Father fed her during the session.

When asked later if he had any ideas at all about Celie's gagging behavior, Father bragged that he had taught Celie this in a game. He also played this game with his nephew who was about the same age as Celie. He demonstrated to the evaluator the gagging game he played with Celie and his nephew. This game with a slight variation was observed later when Father rejoined Celie after a brief absence from the room. She greeted him with a tongue thrust and a gagging sound. When he moved close to her to play with her, she put a doll-figure into her mouth and then extended it to Father's mouth. For a moment he opened his mouth as if to play this reciprocal oral game but then shook his head and said, "Nasty, nasty."

Both parents came from large families in which the mothers were overburdened with the care of children and fathers were absent or unavailable. Mother recalled being rejected by her siblings, and she believed her mother had failed to teach her how to care for herself or her children. The only good relationship she believed she had was with her father who was killed when she was only a year old. She had no memories of him but claimed she had been told he spoiled her. Father was the second of nine children. He reported the babies were all a year apart, and his mother always had a baby to care for and "everybody took care of everybody." His father was a miner and slept during the day. He and his siblings were sent out of the house to play unattended at a nearby playground.

The entire videotape of the parents' session with Celie was made a part of the court record. Edited portions were presented to the court by the parents' attorneys to refute the allegations that Father had sexually abused Celie. The videotape of Celie's approaches to Father and her "tongue-thrust" greeting were parts of the edited sections and were probably the most convincing part of testimony presented to the court. The judge's discomfort in watching little Celie thrust her head into Father's crotch over and over and over was unmistakable.

The court found that Celie had been abused by her parents and ordered no more contact with them. Parental rights were terminated when the parents failed to make progress in treatment.

CONCLUSION

Parents and children give behavioral clues to shared experiences during the interview and observation periods. The behavioral clues are sometimes subtle, but when viewed within the context of the material available in the interview and from other sources reveal the kinds of experiences the child has had with each parent. Observations of unhealthy and abusive parent-child interactions may be critical in establishing parental abuse and in implementing an appropriate treatment program for the child and his or her parents.

9

Children Speak Through Words, Behavior, and Symbolic Play

Children speak through words, behavior, and symbolic play in their interactions with parents and parent-figures. They communicate indirectly what they cannot say directly about their experiences. Recurrent themes emerge in the child's communications with each parent during an observation period; these themes provide insight into the child's experiences with each parent. Careful analysis of patterns of the child's verbal and nonverbal communications in interactions with each parent will show the child's perception of and experiences with each parent and also the child's current conflicts or issues related to the current family situation. A trained evaluator will be able to discern, identify, and demonstrate whether each relationship is healthy.

The child brings a history with each parent into the assessment room; it is this history that gives the assessment observation period its vitality and makes it a paradigm for the ongoing relationships. The child cannot change behaviors on cue even if the parents "perform" for the camera or try to manipulate the child to disguise the true nature of their relationship. Neither the child nor the parents can change their experiences with each other simply because they are being videotaped. The family has a certain set of shared experiences that they bring with them into the session, and they behave in familiar or characteristic ways with each other.

An interactional assessment is not invalidated by separation of the parents and child or by statements made by one parent to discredit the other. The child's experiences with each parent will dictate the child's behavior with that parent.

A child's conflicted feelings about an abusive parent also will be displayed in words and behavior during interactions with that parent. A child may love the parent and want a relationship with that parent despite the abuse, but without the uncomfortable and unhealthy parts of that relationship. The child will demonstrate these feelings.

"STOP, DADDY. DADDY, STOP"

Three-year-old Katie ran into the assessment room where Father was waiting for her. She reached up to hug him as he lifted her into his lap. Katie's greeting appeared enthusiastic; however, closer scrutiny showed her discomfort. Most striking was her failure to make eye contact with Father when she talked with him. When Father kissed her gently on the back of her neck, Katie climbed down from his lap. She asked about the person who normally supervised visits with Father and asked if they could go to the park where the visits normally occurred. Katie was uncomfortable when alone with Father and needed someone to make sure Father did not involve her in games she did not like.

Katie used animal puppets, dinosaurs, and drawings to tell Father she did not like the games he played with her. For example, she screamed at Father, "I'm mad, I'm mad," and then attacked his doggie with her lion puppet. Father asked her why she was mad and then informed her that his doggie was happy. Katie continued to state her lion was mad and again attacked Father's doggie with her lion.

To demonstrate why the lion was mad, Katie gave the lion to Father and took a rabbit puppet for herself. She touched the inside of the rabbit's mouth and asked Father to say what it was. Father said it was a mouth. Katie asked Father what its name was, and when Father said he did not know, Katie asked if it were a dog. Father agreed that it was and greeted it "Hey, dog," as he aggressively grabbed the rabbit's mouth.

Father's reluctance to accurately identify the puppet as a rabbit may have been related to a game he had played with Katie. According to Mother, Katie told her one day that she did not want to be a rabbit anymore and then asked Mother to make Daddy stop. Although Father denied sexually abusing Katie, he recalled that playing "Chomper" was one of his favorite activities with Katie and her older sister, Judy, when she was a toddler. Chomper was a rabbit.

As Father talked about Chomper, Katie, who was playing at the dollhouse, yelled, "Stop, Daddy. Daddy, stop." A few minutes later she left the dollhouse and began to roll Play Doh into an oblong piece. She announced she was "making this like a carrot." Father smiled and asked, "Are you making me a carrot?" Katie said she was making "a big carrot," and when she finished, she took it and dropped it into Father's lap. Judy began to roll a carrot shape as well, and when Katie asked her if she could eat her carrot, Judy said, "No." When Katie asked "Why?" she explained that it was just Play Doh.

Katie played another game with Father that was reminiscent of experiences in which he had put something into her mouth. She took a big dinosaur to Father and asked if it was hungry. When Father said that it was, Katie put her finger into the dinosaur's mouth and instructed Father to do the same. Each time Father said "Ouch." Father spoke for both Katie and himself, as each inserted a finger into the dinosaur's mouth. Katie then picked up a little dinosaur and instructed Father to put his finger in its mouth, telling him to "Put your finger way down in there." When he took his finger out of the dinosaur's mouth, she instructed him to "keep it in there." She asked Father if his finger went all the way down to the dinosaur's tail. The exchange ended with Katie attacking the dinosaur.

Katie continued her efforts to let Father know she did not like what he had done to her. She told him there were monsters in the house, and she would not accept his assurance that there were no monsters. This was followed by getting her father to help her draw a picture (see Figure 16).

She directed him to draw a circle and then to draw another circle. She told him to put a mouth on the little one, and when he drew a mouth with a smile, she complained, "Not a happy one." Katie directed him to "Put some chin," and then as if to make certain Father knew the small circle represented herself, she told him to put lots of hair on the circle, saying, "I have lots of hair." She asked Father to draw a happy mouth on the big circle and also to draw a chin. With the completion of the circles, Katie began to whine and to say that she wanted to go to the park.

Father did not understand what Katie had been trying to communicate to him or thought no one else did. Not surprisingly, when asked where he thought all the concerns about Katie came from, Father said he had no idea and that someone was setting him up. No matter how Father tried to disguise his sexual in-

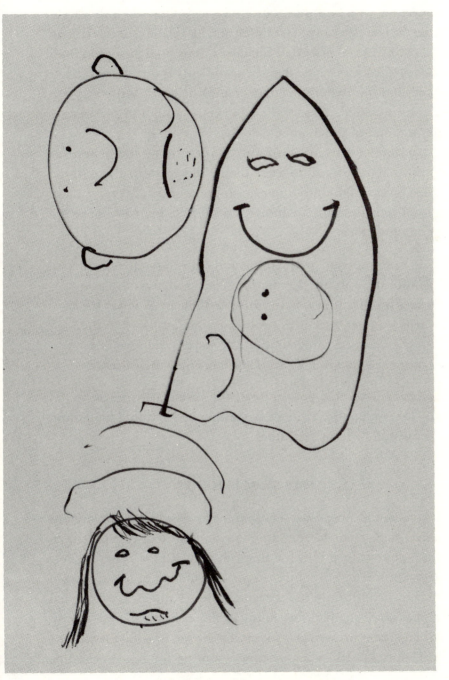

Figure 16. "Not a Happy One"

volvement with both Katie and Judy beginning when they were little, he could not present himself and his relationship with them as healthy. As described in Chapter 6, Judy used metaphors and stories to say indirectly what she could not say directly about her experiences with her stepfather. Katie's behavior and words with Father provided clues to her experiences with him and her anger to him for hurting her.

An abusive parent's response to what he or she believes is important for parents to teach their children or to give to them often gives insight into his or her rationalization of engaging in sexual activities with a minor child. This father's response is a good illustration:

> To enjoy life and go out there and enjoy it for all it's worth and not be afraid of everything, learn what you're gonna need in the future, have fun with their lives, enjoy themselves, enjoy their lives. All things are available to them, enjoy all good things in life. Be happy and love one another. Be happy, have a good time, enjoy their lives.

Father believed the girls enjoyed the sexual activities as he did and also rationalized the sex by viewing it as learning something they would need in the future.

"MY MOM IS HERE"

Four-year-old Amy (also see Chapter 6) was observably anxious about seeing her father, although she had had regular supervised contact with him for almost a year. Clues to her anxiety were abundant, but subtle. Repeated rubbing of her eyes from the moment she entered the room where Father was waiting led him to ask if she had something in her eye or if she was sleepy. When Father pressed her about why she was looking the way she was, Amy said that her mom was waiting for her downstairs.

During the next several minutes she repeatedly mentioned that her mom was in the building and waiting for her. Amy began to scratch her arm, and with Father's curiosity about what was wrong, Amy pointed out an "owie" on her arm. The impression was that Father made her uncomfortable and that physical closeness with him was particularly stressful.

Father, as if aware of Amy's discomfort, suggested that they could do puzzles together. Even with the puzzles, however, Amy's anxiety was apparent. She chose a simple four-piece puzzle and mislabeled the hippopotamus as a dinosaur, although she had correctly labelled it the previous day in the session with Mother. A beaver labelled correctly as a beaver the previous day was now viewed as a bear. All of the animals were scarier on this day with Father.

Amy instructed Father to take the puzzle pieces out with his hand "like me." He replied, "I can't, because my hands are too big" and pointed out that Amy had little bitsy fingers. As if there had been other things that Father had persuaded her she could do better than he, Amy showed how she could "grab" it with her little hands with, "That's how I take it apart." Father encouraged her: "Just pull it right out."

Amy joined with Father in coloring pictures in a coloring book Father had brought. She insisted that they color the pictures upside down and chose to color a lady with a big open mouth. Amy identified the female figure with the large open mouth as herself and identified another picture as Father. When Father asked why that picture was him, Amy said because he had a beard like the man in the picture. Then in a play on words, Amy began to chant,

> You have a beard, last week you gave me a sip of your beer.
> When I was 3 you gave me a sip of your beer. I had a sip of
> your beer, you know that I had a sip of your beer.

When Amy finished her chant, Father asked, "Are you staying in the lines now?" Amy stopped her chanting and complimented Father, "That's very good. You're doing the goodest job in the whole world. I think you're the best dad in the whole world." Amy had confronted Father with a secret they had agreed to keep, and as if she recognized his word of caution to her, she sought to regain his favor by telling him he was the "best dad in the whole world."

Amy, however, needed to let Father know that he had hurt her in the past and used an incident from a recent visit to communicate this to him:

> *Amy:*   Last week when I was at Diane's you were comb-
>   ing my hair when I was leaving.
> *Father:*   Yeh.
> *Amy:*   You shouldn't have did that because that pony-
>   tail hurted.
> *Father:*   Yeh, I know.
> *Amy:*   So I don't like hurt. I like gentle.
> *Father:*   (*ignores this*) Oh I see, I need a bright red.

Father had discounted what she told him about not liking to be hurt, and perhaps recognizing this, Amy again showed signs of discomfort with being physically close to Father. She moved away from him and suggested that they pretend to talk on the telephone by saying, "I'm at my house and you're at your house."

In a game similar to that observed with Katie, Amy used the dinosaurs to tell Father how he had hurt her. While the evaluator was asking Father about what he thought about the allegations that he had sexually abused his daughter, Amy brought the dinosaur to him, pushed it toward him, and told him to look in its mouth. Father looked and also stuck his finger inside the dinosaur's mouth. Amy reassured father, "It won't bite your finger all gone." She then asked, "Did it bite your finger all gone?"

Father answered, "No, I was just playing." Amy then stuck her own finger inside the dinosaur mouth and pretended her finger was all gone.

During this exchange, Father denied there was any truth to the allegations and claimed that his ex-wife was simply using it to limit his access to Amy. He said Amy's statements had been taken out of context, and it was "the old adage of a misplaced comma changes the meaning of the sentence or whole paragraph." He said Amy had slept with him, but it did not have the meaning others had given to it; and that when Amy masturbated she said, "Daddy lets me do it," but that he had told her this was not appropriate to do in public. He complained about the limitations on his current visitation and the effect it would have on his relationship with Amy if it continued for an extended period of time.

Amy sat beside Father and played with an Etch-a-Sketch as Father recalled experiences with her when she was small. Her drawings were instructive about what memories were evoked as Father talked about what would seem to be normal kinds of experiences with a baby. For example, when Father recalled Amy's first smiles, she filled in the Etch-a-Sketch with black. A few minutes later as he talked about the fun things he enjoyed with her, she drew oblong objects on the Etch-a-Sketch and directed Father's attention to them. He responded, "Beautiful."

As if the oblong shapes also reminded him of special experiences with Amy, Father slipped into talking about teaching her things, emphasizing that he never forced her to do things but simply allowed her to utilize her capabilities:

Well I always enjoyed having her around. One thing that also occurred with other children, watching her grow from this little helpless totally dependent thing, every day that goes by, like the second day she was born, she lived twice as long. As I go back, I guess the learning experiences they go through, see how much they can learn and how quickly they can learn. Sometimes you can force them into doing things and sometimes. I never really believed in forcing a child to learn how (*pause*) to walk or anything like that. Maybe never stand them up and force them to do something like that. I figure God knew when she was supposed to walk. They had their own little clock inside them and when it was time for them to get up and walk they'd get up and walk.

Although he tried to provide an example that would normalize the things he allowed but did not force, he was actually rationalizing his own use of Amy—to meet his sexual needs because he never forced her to learn things but simply followed her own "little time clock" and recognized when she had the motor capabilities to do things that gave him pleasure. Later when he compared Amy to his other children, he described her as a "quicker learner." As if showing appreciation for Father's compliment, Amy went to give him a hug.

Father described his own stern stepfather, who used corporal punishment and his mother, to whom he was emotionally but not physically close, although they "hugged each other and things like that." He captured the bleakness of his childhood in the following words:

As far as myself goes, I never had a real childhood; the only way I could describe it, I don't remember, like I never had any toys. It was like this (*points outside—day is overcast and cloudy*); it was gray, rainy days, very little sunshine.

He said that "it was a sunny day" the day his stepfather died. He described his mother as helpless to protect him and also stated that the injuries he suffered as a child were never really life-threatening:

There was never anything that was ever life threatening or severe bodily injuries or anything like that. She probably felt there wasn't much of anything she could do about it.

Amy found excuses to leave before the end of the session. She said her mother was probably ready to go and that she needed to get home to help her mother make muffins. When Amy was gone, the evaluator asked Father if he had any explanation for Amy's disclosure of sexual abuse to her day-care teacher when she was 3 years old. As he explained away Amy's masturbation and each statement she had made to her teacher, Father presented himself as blameless and implied that all the problems were inherent to Amy or the result of her misperception of normal events.

He described her straddling his knee as an infant and rubbing herself and his putting her on the floor to stop it, and a recent time when he noticed her masturbating while laying on his couch and told her this was something to do in private but not in front of other people. He went on to say, "I haven't done anything not in a pleasure-seeking manner." He said he had rubbed "white cream" on Amy when she soiled herself. He said her mother's allegation he was always stealing Amy's panties was not true, that she did not go home with the same pair of panties but always with clean panties. He said the green medicine Amy described was Nyquil he had given her once when she had a cold at his house. He said after that she would beg for the green medicine, and he told her she could only take it when she was sick, when she was "hot."

With all of his careful explanations, this father had created for himself a story that summed up his belief that whatever he had done to Amy had had little effect on her because she did not understand it anyway. He stated it bothered him that Amy's mother had her christened and then elaborated:

It bothered me in a way; when I say it bothered me, it wasn't
that big a deal because Amy doesn't even remember it happening, and nobody else does....I don't know who it was
gonna help. Amy didn't know what was going on. She
didn't like it. (*laughs*) Don't guess that really matters because it only lasts about 30 seconds. She just wound up
with a wet forehead.

The similarity between the child's experience of something wet
on the forehead in a christening and in a sexual experience is
striking. Father seems to be dismissing the significance of any
sexual activity for Amy, who only experienced something wet on
her forehead.

"IS DADDY COMING TODAY?"

Recurrent patterns of behavior both in the sibling session and
in the session with Father showed 4-year-old Rebecca's and 6-
year-old Jason's healthy relationships with their father. This relationship had been disrupted first by Mother's allegations that
Father sexually abused Rebecca when she was 3 years old, and
subsequently by Father's heart attack and Mother's bringing the
allegations a second time when Rebecca was 4.

Rebecca and Jason were observed in a joint play interview
prior to seeing Father. As Rebecca drew a picture of Daddy, she
asked the evaluator, "Is Daddy coming today?" Jason repeated
his sister's question. The evaluator asked the children if they
would like Daddy to come. Rebecca persisted in asking, "Is
Daddy coming today?" while Jason became the chorus that
answered, "No."

The evaluator asked what the children would like to do with
Daddy if he were to come. Without hesitation, Rebecca answered,
"I would like to play with Daddy." The evaluator asked what

they would like to play with Daddy. Each child named an activity that suggested Father's ability to give individual attention to each according to the child's needs and interests. Rebecca responded, "Baby," and Jason answered, "Football."

To explore further what playing "baby" meant for Rebecca, the evaluator asked Rebecca how she played "baby" with Daddy. Rebecca eagerly pointed to the doll with, "Well, there's a baby right there," and announced, "I want to play 'baby' right now." Rebecca picked up the doll and cradled it in her arms to feed it a bottle. Her nurturing behavior with the doll expressed her experiences of being nurtured by Father. Her words to the doll, "She's gonna have her orange juice. Now she's gonna have milk," also reflected her experiences with Father. She was accustomed to Father's efforts to identify her wishes and to give her what she wanted.

A request for the children to draw their family evoked feelings associated with the loss of Father and Jason's anger at his sister for his perception of her role in the loss. Jason became observably less competent as he tried to draw a family that for him no longer existed as an intact family. He dropped the crayon and complained that Rebecca would scribble on his drawing of the family. He angrily threatened, "If she does, she is gonna get it." The implicit message was that Jason blamed Rebecca for causing the trouble that led to loss of Father and did not trust that she would not again do or say something that would disrupt visits with Father.

The children's words and behaviors in the sibling play session showed that each had a healthy relationship with Father uncontaminated by sexual abuse. Their behavior in the first few minutes of reunion corroborated this. Rebecca ran into the room where Father was waiting and literally jumped up into his arms. Jason, who was more reserved, approached Father and patted him on the side as if to get his attention. Father stooped down and placed his arm around Jason to give him a bear hug. Jason abruptly pulled away from Father and ordered Rebecca to "Get off Daddy." Jason's next statement indicated how one ought to interpret his words. He turned to Father and asked, "Do you still have a heart attack?" When Father asked, "Why?" Jason answered, "Because I wanted to jump on you." When Father assured him he was fine and invited him to "Come on, jump," Jason again expressed his concern about Father: "It's gonna hurt." Father assured him, "You can't hurt me," and explained that the longer you go after a heart attack the better it is. During this session, the children used the stethoscope to check out their father's and each other's hearts.

Each child's activity during the session with Father expressed their perception of and experiences with Father. Jason drew a maze and invited Father to play. The object of the game was to get through the maze without running into dead ends. As Father played, he commented that they had to go a different way because someone put a "barrier right in our path." This was symbolic of what had been going on in the family for the past year. As Father and the children were moving toward more normalized relationships after the first allegations of sexual abuse were determined to be unsubstantiated, Mother brought allegations a second time when Father was in intensive care after suffering a heart attack.

Rebecca played "baby" with Father. She gave the doll to Father to hold and then approached with a dinosaur, telling Father that the "animal is going to hurt the baby." Without hesitation, Father assumed a protective role. He held the doll out of reach of the animal and said, "Don't hurt the baby." Rebecca locked the dinosaur and other animals in a cage, saying that they were locked up forever. When Father acknowledged this by saying, "Okay sweetie, now we don't have to worry anymore, do we?" Rebecca replied, "Yes we do," and showed

Father another dinosaur that was not yet locked in the cage. Rebecca's play showed the same theme as Jason's: when one danger is faced and locked away there is no assurance that the danger will not be encountered again. For Rebecca, Father was perceived as the one who could protect the "baby," and for Jason as the one who could find a way around the "barrier."

"DON'T YOU WANT TO GIVE DADDY A HUG?"

Observed patterns of interaction among all family members during reunion illuminate not only the child's experiences with the abusive parent, but also the collusive role of the nonabusive parent. Two-and-one-half-year-old Laura held tightly to the hand of the evaluator as she stood just inside the door where her parents were waiting with her 6-month-old baby brother. Her 18-month-old little sister had run straight to Mother after the evaluator put her down on the floor.

The parents greeted the little girls as if they did not see them as two separate little persons, with "Hi Honeys" and "Hi Sweethearts." As Laura stood with her head bowed, clutching a small doll bottle in her hand, Father tried to engage her and also to explain to the evaluator that her odd behavior was caused by a haircut he had gotten during his one-month separation from them.

Laura's behavior, however, did not indicate she did not know her parents, but rather that she preferred the safety offered by the evaluator to the uncertainty of being with her parents and siblings. When the evaluator asked Laura's permission to leave the room, Laura ran to her mother as if this offered her her only hope of being kept safe from Father.

Of significance is that each little girl ran to Mother on the side away from Father, and each avoided looking at Father or responding to his overtures to them. When Father invited Laura to come give him a hug, Mother asked, "Don't you want to go give daddy a hug?" Laura's answer was unmistakable: she buried her head in Mother's shoulder.

Both little girls lay passive and immobile as Father smiled, talked softly, and gently touched their heads or hands. As if choosing to ignore her daughters' strange reactions to Father, Mother complimented them on how pretty they each were and she herself gave them kisses. She did not inquire what was wrong with them or even acknowledge that something was wrong.

When Father lamented, "Nobody loves Daddy no more," Mother responded, "They've been away from you for so long." The one-month separation did not explain this strong reaction to Father. Father tried to take Sara from Mother but withdrew when Sara pulled away from him and resisted his efforts. As Father stroked Laura's hair, she showed an "owie" on her hand to her mother, who gave it a kiss without inquiring how she got the owie. Father searched for explanations for Laura's reaction to him, asking, "Have they been saying nasty things about your daddy?"; commenting that Laura acted like she was scared of him, that he no longer had his long hair; and apologizing, "I'm sorry you're mad at Daddy."

When Father was unsuccessful in getting Laura to respond to him, Mother placed her on the couch between herself and Father. Laura immediately retreated to Mother and buried her head in Mother's shoulder. Although Mother noticed her discomfort and reassured her, "Mommy's here, I'm not going anywhere," she suggested to Father that they put lotion on the little girls.

As Mother rubbed lotion on Sara's face, Father put lotion on the side of Laura's face exposed to him and then lifted her head to put lotion on the other side of her face. Father then picked Laura up uninvited and hugged and kissed her. Laura did not actively protest but simply lay passive and motionless as Father talked and held her in his arms.

During the next few minutes, Father appeared to check out what Laura remembered and also that she had the capacity to communicate to others. He asked Laura if she still drank from a bottle and whether she could say "Daddy" and "Mommy." As if to communicate to others and also to Daddy that he hurt her, Laura pointed to various "owies" on her body. Father, perhaps to intimidate her, asked if she remembered his dog, a pit bull.

During the clinical interview, Father expressed his belief that "animals are like kids, if you love them and care for them, they———" He did not finish the sentence, but the implication was that he could train children and dogs to do what he wanted and to be loyal to him by making them completely dependent upon him for care.

The process through which he trained the children for participation in sexual activities was observed during the session. For example, during the initial play period prior to the interview, Father suggested to Laura that they get a doll for her to feed. This was not unusual, but his reaction was—when he noticed that the doll he had chosen did not have a hole in its mouth. He commented that the doll did not have a hole in its mouth and turned to Mother to inquire if the doll Sara was playing with had a hole in its mouth. Mother exchanged dolls with Father, and he pointed out to Laura, "See, it's got a hole in its mouth." He fed the doll by pushing the bottle into the hole in its mouth before pushing the bottle nipple into Laura's mouth. Laura pushed the bottle away.

Recall Laura's behavioral reenactment (in Chapter 7) of objects being pushed into the doll's mouth and her own experiences of a penis in her mouth as she squeezed the doll's penis and puffed out her cheeks followed by a gagging sound.

During the clinical interview with the parents, other interactions between the father and each little girl revealed how the father had terrorized them and also had trained them to be submissive and to participate in sexual activities with him. After an uninvited pickup by her father, Laura remained passive and unresponsive in his lap as he kissed and stroked the top of her head. Father ignored Laura's ploy to get out of his lap (she dropped a toy to the floor) and continued to hold her captive in his lap, as if oblivious to the whimpering sounds she made as she sat motionless.

As Laura continued to whimper softly, Mother asked, "What's the matter?" In response to Mother's query, Father reached down to retrieve the toy Laura had dropped. Laura continued to whimper. Mother offered her a Kleenex, and Father helplessly stated that he did not know what he should do to comfort her. Father placed her on the floor, but Laura continued to sob as she stood in the place where Father positioned her. She pointed to her arm and sobbed as if to convey that her arm hurt her. Father lifted her into his lap, and Laura continued to sob. When her sobs escalated to soft crying sounds, Father asked if she wanted to go to Mother, and he took her to Mother. Laura stopped crying and extended her hand to show Mother an "owie." Mother responded as she had earlier; she kissed Laura's hand.

After the above incident, both little girls sat on the couch near Mother and rubbed lotion on each other's bodies. This seemed to be what they did to comfort each other and also what Father did to ease the pain caused by his penetration of their vaginas. Each of the children was being trained individually to please Father with various forms of sexual pleasure, but they were also being trained to participate in sexual games with each other. This training occurred during bathtime, when they were taught to lie on top of each other, and little Jed learned to put his penis into various toys that had holes in them. Even Father's feeding of the doll involved teaching Laura to push the bottle into the *hole* in the doll's mouth and then to put it into her own mouth.

During the clinical interview with the parents, an interaction between Sara and Father showed Father's pleasure in what Sara had learned. As they sat together on the couch facing each other, Father extended his hand with a small oblong object toward Sara's crotch. Sara pushed his hand away, but then she lifted her dress and looked at her crotch. Father sternly commanded, "Put your dress down." His pleasure in her response was displayed in a broad smile, as he seemed to retreat into some fantasy of his own. In her efforts to make a quick escape while Father was distracted, Sara fell onto the floor on her head. Father immediately scooped her up, but as was observed with Laura earlier, nothing he did comforted Sara. Indeed, her screams escalated until Mother took her from Father to offer comfort.

Father reported that his attorney advised him not to participate in the evaluation because his children might act negatively toward him. He seemed to genuinely believe that his children enjoyed the sexual activities as he himself had and would not show a negative reaction to him. He had changed his appearance, however, and hoped to use this as a reason for their negative reaction should this be observed. He explained the children's reaction in the following way:

> My attorney told me it was not good for me to come because the kids might have a negative reaction toward me. Like I said, I've never done anything to my kids except love them. I don't really think they've acted negative towards me. They weren't real sure who I was when they came in....They're not used to seeing a clean-cut dad....I'd probably kill myself if it came to that [loss of children]. Like I said, they are my family. I haven't done anything to my family besides love them. Without them, there would be no reason to go on.

"THE BABY IS SLEEPING"

Father appeared nervous as he waited for 4-year-old Susie and her brothers to join him for the assessment session. He moved to the end of the couch near the doll in the bassinet, leaned over to peer at the doll, poked its stomach, pulled back the blanket, and peered at its face.

Father explained the meaning of this odd behavior a few minutes later when Susie joined him in the room. He repeated his behavior with the doll and asked Susie if she knew what he had been doing. He then explained that he had checked to see if the doll was sleeping, and indeed she was. During the session, he repeated these words and this behavior several more times, as if seeking confirmation from Susie that she was asleep and did not know what happened in the middle of the night.

Recall Susie's behavioral reenactment (Chapter 7) of noises in the night waking the sleeping baby and finally being awakened by a liquid that had been squirted onto the doll's face that was wiped off before she was given a bath. Father wanted to believe (and wanted Susie to believe) that Susie was asleep during the sexual activities that occurred in the night and that she would not have any memory of what happened. Susie's behavioral reenactment in her play session and her words to Father in the presence of her brothers that he hurt her provided her response. Susie was awakened by Father's unusual activities in the middle of the night, and she did remember that he had hurt her and how.

Susie's behavior with Father and her siblings went through various changes across the session. She was visibly anxious when she entered the room and saw Father waiting for her. As the evaluator left the room, she stayed near the door and barricaded herself briefly by pulling two chairs together to make an enclosure. As Father encouraged her to come give him "big hugs and kissers," Susie moved from behind her barricade and, while still maintaining her distance from Father, moved along the wall on the opposite side of the room from where Father was seated on the floor. She lifted her chin as if to show her firm rejection of Father's requests to come give him "big hugs and kissers" and did not reciprocate his statements that he missed her.

During the session, Susie behaviorally showed her vulnerability to and her need for protection from Father's seduction. During the reunion, when Father responded to Susie's statement that they were going somewhere later that day by asking where, Susie defiantly declared, "I'm not telling." However, at the same time, she lifted her dress as though unconsciously exposing herself.

Later she succumbed to Father's seduction, as she participated in the regressed games of giving and receiving open-mouth kisses, and she herself initiated licking her father's face, arms, and hands as if she were a *puppy*. In each instance, she protected herself when Father's words or behaviors evoked memories of his inappropriate behavior with her during unprotected contact. With the regressed games when Father mentioned her coming to his house for a visit, she immediately pulled away from him and with a monotonous, robotlike voice repeated his words. Similarly, when Father again mentioned her visiting him and simultaneously touched her knee, she stopped her licking behavior, and pulling her dress over her knees, she tucked it securely underneath. Although her initial protective stance weakened during the session with Father, she still showed her discomfort when Father's words suggested unprotected contact or his actions were perceived to be intrusive.

At the end of the evaluation series, Susie was able to behaviorally reenact the scary experiences with Father, and later she was able to confront him directly about the hurt that he had inflicted. Although she tried to confront Father in her first session with him, she was not strong enough to be successful. During reunion, as she stood across the room from Father, who was seated on the floor, she asserted, "You hurt me—my mommy's feelings." Father heard and repeated, "You hurt me." Susie, however, repeated "My mommy's feelings." Even though Father asked if she wanted to talk about it, his demeanor suggested this would not be a good idea. When Susie shook her head, Father immediately interpreted this as "No?" and then reminded her of a gift he had given her. This began a pattern of bribes or reminders of gifts Father used whenever Susie rejected his bids for affection or failed to meet his needs during the session.

At the conclusion of the session and after the children were gone, Father described his reaction to seeing Susie after not having seen her for over a year. He said he was happy with Susie's response to him. He stated that she had been told things about him and because of this he had been uncertain about how she might respond to him. Having seen her, he did not think "anything would be adverse" with him and Susie, especially if they had more opportunities for "play and exposure." He then elaborated: "I've got to do some continuing exploration about how it will affect her on down in life, but at her age I think things are reversible." As with other fathers who abuse, he wanted to believe that Susie would not be affected by the abuse since she was small, and that if she did remember he could reverse the ill effects by "play and exposure."

"UNLESS HE JUST STUMBLED INTO IT"

Three-year-old Billy entered the room where Father was waiting in a subdued manner. He had a tentative smile on his face but also had his finger in his mouth. When he approached Father, who was standing near the door, Father stepped back as he greeted him, "Hello, how are you." He did not reach out to

Billy, who then walked past Father to the toys on the other side of the room. Father followed him, and as he sat behind Billy, asked, "You got a hug for me?" When Billy did not respond, Father positioned himself in front of Billy and commented, "You're gonna get right into the toys." When Father picked Billy up uninvited a few minutes later, Billy sat quietly as Father stroked his hair before scooting down as soon as Father withdrew his arm from around his waist.

An exchange with the puppets showed Father's reluctance to participate in games that might remind Billy of games they may have played in other contexts. Father picked up the green frog-puppet and moved it toward Billy's face. When Billy called it a "frog," Father responded, "Is that a frog? I think it's an ostrich." As Billy continued to insist that it was a frog, Father continued with his questioning: "Is he a frog?" When Billy answered that he was a frog, Father said, "I think he's just a funny face." When Billy put his finger in the frog-puppet's mouth, Father playfully bit it. Billy laughed and withdrew his finger. Perhaps stimulated by a game that had meaning for both Billy and Father, Father bounced the nerf ball off Billy's bottom as he asked, "What have you been up to?"

In his play session, when the evaluator asked Billy what had happened, Billy responded, "My peeper broke off." When the evaluator reflected that this must have been scary, Billy said, "Frog did it, frog eat it up, my peeper broked off." When the evaluator asked who hurt his peeper, Billy aggressively threw the frog-puppet away.

Father denied abusing his son Billy. When asked if there was anything that happened to him as a child that he would not want to happen to Billy, he described an incident when he was 6 or 7 that implicitly suggested he may have been sexually abused by someone who took advantage of his vulnerability:

I don't know what it would be (*laughs*) trying to figure out what it might be, something I didn't like in my life. What happened to me? See no reason why it would have to happen to Billy, unless he just stumbled into it (*laughs*). Let's see, yes, there are, can I put my finger on something, no, I had my moments when I was upset, when I felt rejected. I'd like to leave that feeling of rejection, feeling nobody loves me, really getting down on me, being unfair to me, I'll run away, that hurt. I wish that didn't have to happen to Billy, but I don't know how I'm gonna be able to control it. He's gonna, all you can do at that point is hope you're there when he does feel that way.

When asked to recall the time when he felt rejected, he responded:

Sure, now that you bring it up, I don't remember clearly. I remember packing my bag and walking down the street with it over my shoulders. I walked it off, and said I better get back before it's dark. I was 6 or 7 (*covers mouth and becomes observably sad in demeanor*).

As he described his reaction to hearing about a friend's little girl being molested by a stranger, he seemed to describe his feelings as a child molested by someone he did not know: "Helpless, that's what I did feel, basically helpless." He then covered his mouth with his hands as if to protect himself against some intrusive entry.

When asked a few minutes later who might have molested Billy, assuming that something had happened to him, Father repeated, "Who could have done it?" As he continued to ask this question, he gave different answers, saying he did not know who might do such a thing, that anyone would have to be crazy to do this. As he repeated again, "Who did it?" Billy, who was standing near Father, looked up at him and said softly, "You did." Father ignored this, although it was clear he heard this as he nervously said,

> I guess anybody at this point, I guess anybody could have done it. I don't know, I wouldn't have suspected anybody, but if we're going to come to conclusions this happened and no question about whether it happened, then some-body had to do it. You can't have a crime without, without a criminal.

Father seemed to be speaking about the person who hurt him as a child and to question how he could hurt his son in the same way he was hurt when he was a child.

CONCLUSION

The child's behavior in interaction with the parent gives indis-putable confirmation of the kinds of experiences the child has had with the parent. The parent may have been nurturing in some ways, but if that parent has also used the child to meet his emotional or sexual needs, this will be clearly observable also. However, if the parent has responded appropriately and sensi-tively to the child's needs, and has provided nurturance, stimu-lation, and protection for the child, this nurturing relationship will be clearly observable too.

The child's behavior and words give clues to experiences and en-able the evaluator to determine whether the child associates the par-ent with appropriate nurturance, stimulation, and protection or whether the child associates the parent with confusing and traumatic events. During the family session, it will also be observable if one parent was actually abusive and the other parent was a pas-sive accomplice.

Even though an abusive parent may believe that he or she is concealing all signs of inappropriate sexual interest in and involvement with the child, clues to the deviancy will be obvious in the interactions with the child and in responses to questions asked during the clinical interview.

10

Opportunities for the Helping Professions

When correctly performed, the Kempe Interactional Assessment for Parent-Child Sexual Abuse provides clinical and legal professionals with accurate, definitive answers to two threshold questions: *Did the sexual abuse occur, and if it did occur, was the accused parent the perpetrator?* The availability of an assessment procedure that successfully answers these questions, which has been the initial focus of this book, creates opportunities for professionals to help resolve equally compelling issues involving child protection and treatment and to make powerful presentations in legal proceedings.

CHILD PROTECTION OPPORTUNITIES

When an allegation of sexual abuse of a child has been made, the child's protection must be the primary consideration. An initial screening must be performed with the presumption that protective measures shall be enforced unless affirmatively ruled out; the child cannot be left at risk. This is a basic tenet too often forgotten. All contact between the child and the accused parent must be monitored until the assessment is completed and results are available to determine whether or not the abuse occurred. A finding of "inconclusive" cannot be used as a permit to eliminate child protection measures.

If the abuse occurred as alleged, all contact between the abusive parent and the child must be strictly monitored during treatment. Throughout the treatment, helping professionals must remain alert to individual behaviors, interaction patterns, and communications that indicate the risk or presence of continuing abuse. Interactional assessment can provide direction and emphasis to child protection measures. Protective measures may be relaxed only if, and only to the degree that, there is evidence in family interactions—confirmed by the child's verbal and non-verbal languages—that risk of abuse is abating and that the child is safe.

If the abuse did not occur as alleged, or if the child was abused by someone other than the person originally accused, the child needs to be protected from any actual abuser and until there is successful resolution in the family of the consequences of the false or misdirected accusation. Interactional assessment will help define the necessary child protection measures.

TREATMENT OPPORTUNITIES

Once an accurate assessment has been completed, the family and all its members need treatment, whether the allegation is true or not. If an unbiased assessment is to be accomplished, it must not be conducted *for* the child and *against* the parents, as the public and particularly the participants in some cases seem to feel currently, but rather *for the family.*

When an accusation of parent-child sexual abuse is made, everyone in the family needs therapy and each of the family relationships must be tended to whether the allegation is true or not. If the abuse occurred, and the perpetrator was a parent, professionals must conduct a course of therapy to attempt to heal the family members and relationships. If the abuse did not occur, or if the parent was not the perpetrator, professionals must attempt to resolve the problems that caused the accusation and preserve the family. The child's needs must be met, rather than merely treating or removing the abusive parent.

Treatment professionals must treat the entire family in addition to working in individual therapy to heal each family member. The focus of treatment must be the family and the full constellation of family relationships rather than an isolated child or an isolated behavior. Treatment of an isolated parent is not a treatment of the wounded child; treatment of a target parent-child relationship is not treatment of the affected family. Treatment can be found to be successful only when there are clearly observed healthy interaction patterns and absence of unhealthy interaction patterns.

Treatment of the whole family system requires that therapists work together toward the common goal of healing the family and the successful reunion of the wounded child, the abusive parent, and the nonprotective parent. The therapist for each person in the family must not become overidentified with or overly aligned with his or her client. The therapy must be directed toward treating relationships rather than activities. It is not enough to stop the sexually exploitive activities if the dynamics and attitudes that allowed the abuse to occur remain unchanged. The child also suffers if he or she is scapegoated for causing the breakup of the family or if the parent withdraws all affection and care, leaving the child abandoned and lonely (Tyler & Brassard, 1984).

Treatment professionals must learn to communicate with children. Although children do not have all the information that professionals need, they have a wealth of information that is often overlooked because it is not sought or is not recognized when it is obtained.

Children can and do speak for themselves in the treatment, as well as in the assessment, process. Treatment professionals must permit and encourage them to do so (James, 1989). Treatment professionals must be trained in play therapy techniques and must have the skills to observe and to interpret the child's behavior. The treatment must be designed to permit the child to actively participate and express him or herself. It must address the child's victimization but also must allow the child to explore conflicted feelings about the abusive parent. The child may wish for the parent to get help also and to have a relationship that is uncontaminated by abuse or by the uncomfortable experiences.

Treatment professionals must learn to communicate with each other. All professionals involved in the treatment process (e.g., mental health, medical, education, legal) must act in concert. Often it is not a lack of skill that stops professionals from offering or accepting guidance and participating with each other but rather timidity, confusion, lack of access, and inadequate backup. Family treatment, based on the Kempe Interactional Assessment, provides ample opportunity for concerted efforts among the professionals.

SYSTEM OPPORTUNITIES

Early preventive identification and treatment may be possible based on assessment of family relationships (Haynes-Seman & Krugman, 1989). We need to anticipate, expect, fund, and staff long-term intervention when necessary. We need to eliminate labels that lead to narrow assessment and treatment perspectives (e.g., "dependent and neglected" versus "family in need of services"). We need to integrate legal, mental health, medical, education, and social services, so that we are not dealing with separate "cases" but with a family. We need consistency among intervention processes.

If we presume to intervene with a family, we must treat the whole family. We need trained and experienced specialists, such as lawyers who are knowledgeable about children, their needs, and healthy parent-child relationships. We need a framework that is accepted in the professional community by consensus for how we view parent-child sexual abuse. An assessment consensus can then be obtained. There is no excuse not to find out the truth; the *unsubstantiated* must be followed through until proved true or false. This can be accomplished only through evaluation of the whole family and of relationships within the family, past and present. Verbal disclosure of the child or confession of the abusive parent must not be the only proof accepted by professionals or the courts.

PRESENTATION IN COURT

A helping professional who participates in or relies upon an interactional assessment will gain a vital skill, and some measure of comfort, by understanding the rudiments of presenting expert evidence and testimony in an adversarial legal proceeding.

There are two legal tests that historically courts have used to evaluate whether testimony offered by the professionals would be admitted as expert evidence. The first test, the Frye Test, set out in 1923 in *Frye v. United States*, 293 F. 1013 (D.C. Cir. 1923), has been the traditional and most widely used way of judging the admissibility of scientific evidence. It is also the more difficult to satisfy and more stringent of the tests. Its rationale is that scientific evidence should not be admitted unless the principles on which the underlying procedure is based are "sufficiently established to have gained general acceptance in the particular field in which it belongs" (*Frye* at 1014). The second test is set out in the Federal Rules of Evidence, Rule 702, which allows the introduction of "scientific, technical or other specialized knowledge [if it] will assist the trier of fact to understand the evidence or to determine a fact in issue." The trial court will ask the following question: "On this subject can the fact-finder [i.e., a judge or jury] from this person receive appreciable help?" The Federal Rules of Evidence 702 Test is easier to satisfy than the *Frye* Test.

A threshold determination has been made by each court of which of the two tests to apply to offered testimony. In most states the rule is that the *Frye* Test should be applied "to novel scientific devices and processes involving the manipulation of physical evidence" (e.g., polygraph exams, blood typing, microscopic exams of evidence, voice-print analysis). See *People v. Hampton*, 746 P.2.d 947, 950 (Colo. 1987). Scientific evidence that does not fit the "manipulation of physical evidence" description should be evaluated by F.R.E. 702.

Although interactional assessment is not the novel manipulation of physical evidence type of process that has been subject to the *Frye* Test, and although, in 1993, the United States Supreme Court in the case of Daubert v. Merrell Dow Pharmaceuticals, ____ U.S. ____, 113 S.Ct. 2786(1993), ruled that the F.R.E. 702 test supplanted what the Court called the "austere" *Frye* test, a helping professional should be prepared for the three underlying questions that would be raised by the stringent *Frye* analysis:

1. Is there a theory that supports the conclusions that interactional assessment can produce reliable results? (*See Chapters 1 and 2*)

2. Are there generally accepted interview, observation, and review techniques capable of producing reliable results? (*See Chapters 2 and 3*)
3. Have the accepted techniques been used in this case at hand?

Once the helping professional is established as an expert, the professional's tasks are to present clear, complete, and persuasive testimony.

The professional must be prepared to quickly and efficiently present to the judge and jury the academic and clinical underpinnings of interactional assessments, and the rationale, skills, techniques, and protocol used in the evaluation process. Of equal importance, the professional, by behavior on the stand as well as through the content of testimony, can and should engage the judge and jurors as active participants in a search for the truth rather than as passive observers; professionals must teach the judge and jury how to observe, what to observe, and the significance of what is observed.

In a matter as charged as allegations of sexual abuse of a child, the judge and jury must be helped to recognize their individual biases and strong emotions that may cause them difficulty in accepting and acting upon information presented to them. Whether these biases and emotions stem from personal history or social morals, the professional may help defuse them by building trust and confidence with the judge and jury that interactional assessment is based on common experiences and common sense. An effective aid to this process is the professional's written report that a judge or jury may examine as evidence; it must contain all of the data and not just the conclusions. It should outline all of the components of the assessment, including the noncase specific "how-to's" and protocol.

Videotapes, such as those produced in an interactional assessment, when properly authenticated and relevant, are admissible in evidence. They are an essential and powerful tool. Sufficient work and conversation with counsel will ensure that evidentiary prerequisites can be met for admissibility of the videotapes in their entirety; admissibility of the videotapes with excerpted edits, if desired; and admissibility of the videotapes with narrated voice-over. Authentication may require testimony as to the circumstances surrounding the taking of the videotape—which may include evidence that the parents signed an informed consent for the session to be videotaped and that the video accurately depicts the events that occurred. The accuracy of an edited videotape can be established by availability of the unedited videotapes to the court prior to hearing.

Finally, but of paramount importance, the professional must establish credibility by demonstration that he or she is an expert committed to finding the truth, that is, the expert has no bias to a particular outcome (or to finding or not finding pathology); the expert made no predetermination of a particular outcome; the expert examined all available evidence whether favorable to the ultimate conclusion or not; and the expert's conclusion is the result of a complete process in which no evidence is disregarded.

CONCLUSION

The Kempe Interactional Assessment is a complete and accurate process that provides objective and definitive evidence regarding allegations of parent-child sexual abuse. It is a unique aid in responding to fundamental challenges presented to clinical and legal professionals caused by allegations of parent-child sexual abuse.

References

Ainsworth, M. D. S., & Wittig, B. (1969). Attachment and exploratory behavior of one-year-olds in a strange situation. In B. M. Foss (Ed.), *Determinants of infant behaviour*, Vol. IV (pp. 111–136), London: Methuen.

American Academy of Child and Adolescent Psychiatry (1990). *Policy Statement from the American Academy of Child and Adolescent Psychiatry: Guidelines for the clinical evaluation of child and adolescent sexual abuse.* Approved by Council of the AACAP, June 10, 1988. Modified December 14, 1990. Washington, DC: AACAP.

American Professional Society on the Abuse of Children (1990). *Guidelines for psychosocial evaluation of suspected sexual abuse in young children.* APSAC Task Force on the Psychosocial Evaluation of Suspected Sexual Abuse in Young Children, Chaired by Lucy Berliner, MSW. Chicago: APSAC.

Angelou, Maya. (1993). *On the pulse of morning.* New York: Random House.

Benedek, E. P., & Schetky, D. H. (1985). Allegations of sexual abuse in child custody and visitation disputes. In D. H. Schetky & E. P. Benedek (Eds.), *Emerging issues in child psychiatry and the law* (pp. 145–156). New York: Brunner/Mazel.

Berliner, L., & Conte, J. R. (1993). Sexual abuse evaluations: Conceptual and empirical obstacles. *Child Abuse & Neglect, 17,* 111–125.

Bowlby, J. (1969). *Attachment and loss* (Vol. 1). New York: Basic Books.

Bowlby, J. (1988). Developmental psychiatry comes of age. *American Journal of Psychiatry, 145,* 1–10.

Bresee, P., Stearns, G. B., Bess, B. H., & Packer, L. S. (1986). Allegations of child sexual abuse in child custody disputes: A therapeutic assessment model. *American Journal of Orthopsychiatry, 56,* 560–569.

Burgess, A. W., & Hartman, C. R. (1993). Children's drawings. *Child Abuse & Neglect, 17,* 161–168.

D'Antonio, M. (1992, October). Words that hurt: The emotional price of verbal abuse. *Child, 7*(8), 108–109, 144, 147, 149.

Dietrich-McClean, G., & Walden, T. (1988). Distinguishing teaching interactions of physically abusive from non-abusive parent-child dyads. *Child Abuse & Neglect, 12,* 469–479.

Di Leo, J. H. (1983). *Interpreting children's drawings.* New York: Brunner/ Mazel.

Egeland, B., & Sroufe, A. (1981). Attachment and early maltreatment. *Child Development, 52,* 44–52.

Everson, M. D., & Boat, B. (1989). False allegations of sexual abuse by children and adolescents. *Journal of American Academy of Child and Adolescent Psychiatry, 28,* 230–235.

Finkelhor, D., & Browne, A. (1985). The traumatic impact of child sexual abuse: A conceptualization. *American Journal of Orthopsychiatry, 55,* 530–541.

Finkelhor, D., Hotaling, G. T., Lewis, I. A., & Smith, C. (1990). Sexual abuse in a national survey of adult men and women: Prevalence, characteristics, and risk factors. *Child Abuse & Neglect, 14,* 19–28.

Fraiberg, S. (Ed.) (1980). *Clinical studies in infant mental health: The first year of life.* New York: Basic Books.

Freud, S. (1953). Preface to the fourth edition of three essays on the theory of sexuality. In J. Strachey (Ed. and trans.), *The Standard Edition of the complete psychological works of Sigmund Freud* (Vol. 7, p. 133). London: Hogarth Press. (Original essays published 1905; fourth edition published 1920.)

Furchner, J. (1989). Respecting the child's eye view. *Preventing Sexual Abuse, 2,* 8–12.

Furth, G. M. (1988). *The secret world of drawings: Healing through art.* Boston: Sigo Press.

Gaddini, R. (1983). Incest as a developmental failure. *Child Abuse & Neglect, 7,* 357–358.

Green, A. H. (1986). True and false allegations of sexual abuse in child custody disputes. *Journal of the American Academy of Child Psychiatry, 25,* 449–456.

Haynes-Seman, C., & Krugman, R. D. (1989). Sexualized attention: Normal interaction or precursor to sexual abuse? *American Journal of Orthopsychiatry, 59,* 238–245.

James, B. (1989). *Treating traumatized children: New insights and creative interventions.* Lexington, MA: Lexington Books, D.C. Heath and Company.

Jones, D. P. H., & McQuiston, M. (1988). *Interviewing the sexually abused child.* London: Gaskell Psychiatry Series.

Kaplan, S., & Kaplan, S. (1981). The child's accusation of sexual abuse during a divorce and custody struggle. *The Hillsdale Journal of*

Clinical Psychiatry, 3, 81–95.

Kellogg, R. (1970). *Analyzing children's art.* Palo Alto, CA: Mayfield Publishing Company.

Kohut, H. (1977). *The restoration of the self.* New York: International Universities Press.

Lidz, T. (1968). *The person: His development throughout the life cycle.* New York: Basic Books.

Main, M., & Goldwyn, R. (1984). Predicting rejection of the infant from mother's representation of her own experience: Implications for the abused-abusing intergenerational cycle. *Child Abuse & Neglect, 8,* 203–217.

Schetky, D. H. (1991). The sexual abuse of infants and toddlers. In A. Tasman & S. M. Goldfinger (Eds.), *Review of psychiatry,* Vol. 10 (pp. 308–319). Washington, DC: American Psychiatric Press.

Sorensen, T., & Snow, B. (1991). How children tell: The process of disclosure in child sexual abuse. *Child Welfare, 70,* 3–15.

Starr, R. H. (1987). Clinical judgement of abuse-proneness based on parent-child interactions. *Child Abuse & Neglect, 11,* 87–92.

Stechler, G., & Halton, A. (1987). The emergence of assertion and aggression during infancy: A psychoanalytic systems approach. *Journal of the American Psychoanalytic Association, 35,* 821–838.

Steele, B. F. (1970). Generational repetition of the maltreatment of children. In E. J. Anthony & G. H. Pollock (Eds.), *Parental influences in health and disease* (pp. 121–133). Boston: Little, Brown.

Steele, B. F. (1980). Psychodynamic factors in child abuse. In C. H. Kempe & R. E. Helfer (Eds.), *The battered child,* Third Edition (pp. 49–85). Chicago: The University of Chicago Press.

Steele, B. F. (1983). The effect of abuse and neglect on psychological development. In J. D. Call, E. Galenson, & R. L. Tyson (Eds.), *Frontiers of infant psychiatry* (pp. 235–244). New York: Basic Books.

Steele, B. F. (1991). The psychopathology of incest participants. In S. Kramer & S. Akhtar (Eds.), *The trauma of transgression: Psychotherapy of incest victims* (pp. 14–56). Northvale, NJ: Jason Aronson.

Summit, R. (1983). The child sexual abuse accommodation syndrome. *Child Abuse & Neglect, 7,* 177–193.

Tyler, A. H., & Brassard, M. R. (1984). Abuse in the investigation and treatment of intrafamilial child sexual abuse. *Child Abuse & Neglect, 8,* 47–53.

Yates, A. (1991). False and mistaken allegations of sexual abuse. In A. Tasman & S. M. Goldfinger (Eds.), *Review of psychiatry,* Vol. 10 (pp. 320–335). Washington, DC: American Psychiatric Press.

Index